Dale Ralph Davis scores another win with his
Rascal: The Jacob Narrative in book to help preachers and B out of Jacob's stories. But also, up their hearts to a faithful, dur family, and knows how to save despite themselves. Davis will leave readers and disciples with more hope than they've had in ages. But he will similarly draw them deeper into the loving correction of a Father who cares about us too much to leave us mired in our messes. *God's Rascal* is just the book for all of God's rascally people.

Michael W. Philliber
Senior Pastor, Heritage Presbyterian Church,
Oklahoma City, Oklahoma
Author of *Our Heads On Straight* and *To You I Lift Up My Soul*

Dale Ralph Davis models biblical exposition at its best, bringing us into the world of the Bible and applying the Scriptures to our lives today. *God's Rascal* is filled with fresh insights and compelling stories, but most of all, it shows how God's grace prevails, even in the lives of His most troubled children.

Colin S. Smith
Senior Pastor, The Orchard Evangelical Free Church, Arlington Heights, Illinois
Founder and Bible Teacher, Open the Bible, openthebible.org

I am forever in debt to the Lord for Ralph's teaching, which liberated me to honestly present God's Word to His people. Back in the day at Belhaven college where Ralph was our Old Testament professor, he introduced his students to the 'great big God of the Bible' with whom so many of us fell in love and have been forever changed. *God's Rascal* is just a taste of Dr. D's clever whit, rich illustrations, expositional precision as well as his gift for explaining a text in ways that engages both biblical scholar and everyday man in the streets. Every pastor would benefit from having Dr. Davis' collection in his library.

Pat Davey

Assistant Pastor, Eastern Shore Presbyterian Church,
Fairhope, Alabama

God's Rascal is vintage Davis. Whether you are a first-timer to Ralph's expositions or a groupie like me, you will greatly benefit from this book on Genesis 25-35. As you work your way through it you will find that you are constantly reminded of the covenant promises that God first gave to Abraham. The exposition is written in light of these promises; in fact, this is the best way to read this text.

Yes, you will find help for some of the 'troubling texts' that appear in the Jacob narrative. But more importantly, you will see how God's sovereign plan will not be thwarted in Jacob's life, in spite of his sins, and those of his parents, and his brother and father-in-law, and I almost forgot: his wives! Jacob is indeed 'God's Rascal,' but he is a rascal saved by grace. We see him grow in grace, but also see him falter, so we can all relate to him. None of us are in Jacob's position as a significant 'covenant player.' And yet Ralph shows how these texts can rightly apply to the ordinary Christian like you and me. I say unapologetically that Ralph will preach to you in these pages, but that will be good for you. I know it was good for me.

Chris O'Brien

Pastor, First Presbyterian Church, Picayune, Mississippi

GOD'S RASCAL

The Jacob Narrative
in Genesis 25-35

Dale Ralph Davis

CONTENTS

ABBREVIATIONS

ESV	English Standard Version
HCSB	Holman Christian Standard Bible
IVPBBC	The IVP Bible Background Commentary: Old Testament
JB	The Jerusalem Bible (1966)
NAC	New American Commentary
NET	New English Translation
NIB	The New Interpreter's Bible
NICOT	New International Commentary on the Old Testament
NIV	New International Version
NJPS	A New Translation of the Holy Scriptures according to the Traditional Hebrew Text (1985)
TEV	Today's English Version
TOTC	Tyndale Old Testament Commentaries
TWOT	Theological Wordbook of the Old Testament
WBC	Word Biblical Commentary
ZIBBC	Zondervan Illustrated Bible Background Commentary

PREFACE

I want to thank the congregation of Dayspring Presbyterian Church, Forsyth, Georgia, and Pastor David Martin for the invitation to preach from the Jacob narrative at their 2021 spring Bible conference. Those expositions followed a different format than those that follow, but the time spent re-studying Genesis 25–35 stirred my interest; I couldn't quite let go of these chapters, decided to try writing, and, like Aaron's calf (Exod. 32:24), out came this book! It is of similar ilk to *Faith of Our Father* (Gen. 12-25).

For the most part I've tried to steer clear of undue technicalities. The biblical translations are my own unless marked otherwise. I realize I have re-used several illustrations from past expositions but make no apology for that. For one thing, I don't assume readers have read all my previous 'stuff'; for another, even if they have, they've probably forgotten the illustrations. So there you have it.

I should explain that I frequently refer to 'the writer' of the text. I am simply accustomed to speaking that way when dealing with biblical narrative. There may be some suspicious character out there in Bible-exposition-land who suspects I'm trying to avoid affirming Mosaic authorship. Not guilty. Of course, Genesis is anonymous. However, I cannot conceive of any other than Moses as being the primary author and composer of the material. If need be, see the fine discussion in Richard P. Belcher, Jr., *Genesis: The Beginning of God's Plan of Salvation* (Christian Focus, 2012), pp. 14-20.

This modest exposition comes as a tribute to our grandson, Joshua. Like and yet unlike Jacob, he faces life with his own set of challenges and yet not without his own slice of humor. We exchange maybe monthly e-mails, and he usually signs off with 'All the best from your favorite grandchild.' He's pushing the envelope; there are, after all, four granddaughters in the connection. But when I write him back, I sign off with something like, 'Grace and gusto to my favorite grandson.' I can say that without falling into the abyss of Jacob-like favoritism. At any rate, this book is for Joshua.

Dale Ralph Davis

SETTING THE STAGE

Martyn Lloyd-Jones was once recalling some of the striking characters in Llangeitho, the Welsh village of his youth. There was the shoemaker whose shop was always full – and he was apparently available for counsel. A farmer came to him in some anguish. The farmer's oldest daughter had failed an exam at the Intermediate School and was heartbroken. She'd failed before and always in the same subject – algebra. So her father comes to the shoemaker and asks, 'What is this "algebra" that the lass always fails in?' 'Oh! Algebra!' the shoemaker knowingly responds. 'Think now of a train leaving Aberystwyth with thirty passengers on it. It comes to Llanrhystyd Road and two get out and one steps in. On arriving at Llanilar, three get out and no one enters. Tregaron, five get off and six enter. Then from station to station until they arrive at Bronwydd Arms where twelve enter. At last the train reaches Carmarthen. Now this is the problem, this is the question – what was the guard's name?' The farmer immediately understands why his daughter fails and goes home to sympathize with her.[1] Only a unique character would think to explain algebra like that!

And in the biblical materials Jacob certainly ranks as one of the more fascinating characters. He seems like such a

---

1. Iain H. Murray, *The Life of D. Martyn Lloyd-Jones 1899-1981* (Edinburgh: Banner of Truth, 2013), p. 10.

kaleidoscopic blend of deviousness and doggedness, of trickery and tenacity, of folly and faith. I am not 'hot' on focusing on biblical characters, mainly because the text presses us to focus on God and what He is up to. Yet it's hard to avoid Jacob – he sort of forces you to notice him!

But Jacob is a rascal. I don't mean 'rascal' in the popular sense, as of a mischievous child, but in the more original sense of a scoundrel or rogue.

Novelist Bernard Cornwell was once responding to questions from readers of his 'Richard Sharpe' series. Cornwell's Sharpe was not always the epitome of virtue, and one of his readers asked about that – Sharpe is the protagonist and yet he is something of a rogue. Cornwell agreed with the reader but added, 'Yes, but he's *our* rogue.' That supposedly made a bit of a difference.

It seems to me that that is how we find ourselves regarding Jacob. We might not ever want him for our next-door neighbor nor as an honorary uncle for our kids, but, for all that, we still can't help 'pulling' for him in his dilemmas and debacles throughout the story. He's somehow *our* rogue, God's rascal.

1

A Brouhaha in the Making
(Genesis 25:19-34)

Sometimes one catches glimpses of trouble that will not fully erupt until much later. For example, in my own country (USA), Patrick Henry, one of its slave-owning founding fathers, admitted that slavery contradicted the ideals of the American Revolution. And in 1790 James Madison called slavery a 'deep-rooted abuse' and the arguments used to support slavery 'shamefully indecent'.[1] Long before 1861 and the bloodshed of the War Between the States, there was already, at least among some, an 'uneasy conscience' over slavery; there were indicators of what might be coming down the road. Likewise, here in this text one doesn't see the 'brouhaha' yet – only the ingredients that indicate it is coming: fetuses smashing each other in the womb (v. 22), parental favoritism (v. 28), and the birthright sale (vv. 29-34).

Here at 25:19 we arrive at the 'generations' of Isaac. The word is *toledoth* and it occurs over ten times in Genesis in

---

1. Thomas S. Kidd, *American History, Volume 1* (Nashville: B & H Academic, 2019), p. 69; and Larry Schweikart and Michael Allen, *A Patriot's History of the United States* (New York: Sentinel, 2004), p. 115.

headings like this. 'Generations' doesn't convey the sense very well. The word is from the root *yalad* (to bear, beget, give birth) and refers to what is produced or what develops from a person. So the *toledoth* of Isaac here does not have much to do with Isaac (except a bit here and in chapter 26) but primarily refers to what *developed* from Isaac, namely Jacob and matters relating to him. So too in 37:2, when the text speaks of 'the *toledoth* of Jacob,' the focus is on Joseph and his brothers – i.e., what developed out of Jacob. Something like 'developing story' or 'ensuing story' might best capture the idea.[2] In any case, 'the *toledoth* of Isaac' takes in 25:19–35:29 and mostly focuses on Jacob. This is our chunk of text. More specifically, now we focus on 25:19-34 and simply want to ask what it is that we are meant to see here.

First off, we run into **the typical difficulties of God's people** (vv. 19-21). Here are Isaac and Rebekah, but Rebekah is 'barren' (v. 21). Looks like a re-run. Sarah was barren (11:30) and it took up ten chapters of Genesis before Isaac was born (chapter 21). Now Rebekah repeats the pattern. And it's really difficult to become a 'great nation' (12:2) without a biological starter kit. Unlike Abraham and Sarah, Isaac and Rebekah do not use some facsimile of the 'Hagar method' (chapter 16). Instead Isaac resorts to prayer (v. 21a). John Currid notes that the Hebrew terminology indicates that Isaac did more than pray 'for' his wife, but that he prayed 'in front of' her, in her presence.[3] Yahweh granted the request; Rebekah becomes pregnant. Verse 20 says that Isaac was forty when he married Rebekah, and verse 26 says he was sixty when the twins were born – hence twenty long years of childlessness.

---

2. Cf. TWOT, 1:380.

3. John D. Currid, *A Study Commentary on Genesis*, 2 vols. (Darlington: Evangelical Press, 2003), 2:12.

At this point you should glance at the *context*. Look at 25:12-18, 'the *toledoth* of Ishmael.' Granted, it's not the greatest devotional section; you are not particularly fascinated with Mishma, Dumah, and Massa, for example. But do you see the stark contrast? Here is the non-chosen line of Ishmael with twelve sons; Ishmael's line has fertility coming out of its ears. Isaac's line can't even become a line until, after twenty years, there is one conception. How often it seems that the prospects for the people of God in this world are pretty hopeless.

James Humes asks us to imagine interviewing a job applicant. The young man sitting in front of you not only stutters but has a lisp. You look at his resume and find he has no college degree, in fact has never attended college. Then you hear from an associate that this fellow had fainted out of fear in one of his first public appearances.[4] He's referring to Winston Churchill, but at that point things looked pretty bleak. And the writer's point here is that the people of God in this world often seem like that – weak and fragile and apparently fruitless and of little account, an unimpressive lot. That is so often still the case for Christ's church. The Belgic Confession (1561) captures both the hope but also the realism in this:

> This Church has existed from the beginning of the world and will be to the end, for Christ is an eternal King who cannot be without subjects. This holy Church is preserved by God against the fury of the whole world, *although for a while it may look very small and as extinct in the eyes of man* (From Article 27; emphasis mine).

'Very small and as extinct' – but *there*. God so frequently begins His work with next to nothing and continues it in repeated episodes of apparent hopelessness.

---

4. James C. Humes, *The Sir Winston Method* (New York: William Morrow, 1991), p. 15

Secondly, we see here **the surprising announcement of God's decision** (vv. 22-23). Well, it was a nasty pregnancy. The lads 'kept smashing one another' in the womb (v. 22a). One is tempted to offer Rebekah some comfort with: 'They're not kicking you, Rebekah, they're punching one another.' It causes Rebekah much anguish and distress. Her question in verse 22b is choppy and hard to translate. One wonders if the pain affected her coherence. Why this kind of pregnancy? She's baffled and goes to 'inquire of Yahweh' (v. 22c). Who knows what that involved? Did she go to some prophet? A priest? At any rate, Yahweh's answer was:

> Two nations are in your womb,
> and two peoples coming out of you will be divided;
> and one people will be stronger than the other
> – and the older will serve the younger (v. 23).

The twist comes in the climactic line – a reversal of the expected. Yahweh tends to be unconventional; He does not necessarily follow society's expectations or kowtow to its standards. 'The older will serve the younger.' Paul picks up on this in Romans 9:10-12, underscoring what a sheer sovereign decision it was – declared before their births, before either had done any actual good or bad. God does not have to consult us; His decisions are not subject to our discussion.

I know I have alluded to it somewhere before, but this 'sovereignty' brings to mind that anecdote Seymour Morris, Jr., tells of Abraham Lincoln. Seems President Lincoln was finding himself at odds with his cabinet over some matter under debate. So, at the end of the disagreement he was tallying up how things stood: 'Seven nays, one aye; the ayes have it.' He could say how it would be, because, after all, he was the president.[5]

There is that 'sovereign' note in this text (v. 23d) – and it is a sovereignty that goes against the stream, against the way

---

5. In *American History Revised* (New York: Broadway, 2010), p. 232.

man would normally do things. What we must see is that it's only because of this unconventional pattern in God's ways that we have hope. You remember how Paul speaks of this in 1 Corinthians? What he calls 'the foolishness of God'? He tells the Corinthians to look around at themselves – they will not find many wise by human standards, not many mighty, not many bluebloods. And why? Because 'God chose the foolish things of the world ..., God chose the weak things of the world ..., and God chose the insignificant things ... the despised things, the things that are nothing ...' (1:27-28). So we have hope because of this surprising, sovereign God.

Next, I think the writer also wants us to see **the natural folly of God's servants** (vv. 27-28). The twins' births are recorded, but the next note (v. 27) introduces them as grown-ups ('Now when the lads had grown up ...'). Gobs of time and experiences are omitted. The writer doesn't provide a detailed biography but only notes what we need to know. And apparently, we need to know that Esau was an expert hunter, an outdoorsman, and that Jacob may've been more of a homebody, perhaps focusing on livestock. In any case, we're told that Isaac loved Esau because he was addicted to the game Esau killed and cooked up, while Rebekah loved Jacob (v. 28). Apparently, this was obvious. This favoritism will bring on trouble come chapter 27 – just as Jacob's favoritism will in chapter 37.

Kulula Airlines used to have a take-off on one of those traditional airline announcements: 'In the unlikely event of a sudden loss of cabin pressure, an oxygen mask will drop down ...' The announcement goes on to instruct anyone traveling with a child to arrange one's own mask first before tending to the child's. Then Kulula raised the ultimate dilemma: 'If you're traveling with more than one child, pick your favorite!' Isaac and Rebekah would be in no doubt of theirs.

Isn't the text raising a blinking yellow light about parental favoritism? Isn't it implying that we need to exercise wisdom in this matter? Some interpreters might say that we need to keep our eyes on what 'preaches Christ' in an Old Testament text and not get caught up in moralistic points. No, we don't want to bog down in some morass of moralism, only looking for lessons or examples that we can pull out of an Old Testament narrative. But what if such a passage *wants to make* a moral or ethical or exemplary point? If the writer doesn't want to do so, then why did he include verses 27-28? They certainly don't 'preach Christ' as 'Christocentric' interpreters much prefer. Are these verses, however, meant as a warning to covenant people to avoid such folly in their own households? It can be easy to slip into such a practice – it's such a *natural* folly. So shouldn't the text goad us to prayer? Shouldn't we be begging the Lord to keep us from doing anything so blatantly stupid in the life of our family?

Lastly, our chapter highlights **the casual attitude toward God's gifts** (vv. 29-34). Here we zero in on Esau.

I've already noted how verse 27 immediately skipped to the twins' grown-up years – and verses 29-34 provide, at this point, but one anecdote from that time. Jacob is cooking and Esau has been hunting; Esau comes in 'famished' (v. 29b). Just how famished 'famished' connotes we'll have to wait and see. Esau begs, 'Let me gulp down some of the red stuff, this red stuff, for I'm famished' (v. 30). Esau sees stew, Jacob sees opportunity. So Jacob sets a price on the stew: 'Sell me right now your birthright' (v. 31). Esau claims he is 'about to die,' what possible use would a birthright be to him? (v. 32). But Jacob won't budge – he wants Esau to make it 'legal' – to go on oath about it – and he does (v. 33). And stew is served.

This 'birthright' normally belonged to the first-born, though it was transferable, and – at least later in Israel (Deut. 21:17) – involved receiving a double portion of the inheritance; he would also assume family leadership upon the father's death.[6] It entailed both provision and position. The 'blessing' (see chapter 27) was distinct from the birthright; however, the birthright seems to have been the normal pathway to the blessing.

How are we to construe this incident? It's easy for some expositors to malign Jacob for taking unfair advantage of Esau in the latter's dire distress. But just how 'dire' was Esau's distress? If he is 'famished' (vv. 29, 30), does that mean on the brink of starvation or simply that he's terribly hungry? In the same way, is his 'I'm about to die' (v. 32) a statement of literal and imminent fact or a piece of hyperbole similar to some of ours? The post-stew verbs in verse 34 suggest Esau's condition was not so catastrophic: 'so he ate and drank and got up and went on his way.' If anything, they imply a rather casual, nonchalant, business-as-usual demeanor. At any rate, we don't have to guess because the writer himself gives us the authorized interpretation in verse 34b: 'So Esau despised the birthright.' That is how we are to look at it. He didn't give a rip. The problem is not the conniving of Jacob but the apathy of Esau. He may carry on later (27:36) but the writer knows where the blame belongs.

Perhaps the situation is analogous to that of the much-lauded missionary-explorer, David Livingstone. He married Mary Moffat, apparently not out of romantic passion, for he described her as 'sturdy' and 'matter-of-fact.' In something like a half-dozen years, through their various journeys, she delivered five children. She gave birth to the fifth in September 1851, and in his journal Livingstone bemoaned her 'frequent pregnancies.'[7] And we must be pardoned for asking, 'Who, pray tell, was responsible for those?' In like manner, our text

6. See Currid, 2:21; and B. K. Waltke, *Genesis: A Commentary* (Grand Rapids: Zondervan, 2001), pp. 363-64.

7. Ruth A. Tucker, *From Jerusalem to Irian Jaya*, 2nd ed. (Grand Rapids: Zondervan, 2004), pp. 158-59.

here says that Esau was 'to blame.' The writer of Hebrews agrees and when he recalls that Esau 'sold his birthright for a single meal', he calls him 'profane' (*bebelos*, Heb. 12:16). I recall hearing Dr. J. O. Buswell remark that he would translate the term as 'secular.' That was the problem. Esau's style of life didn't really matter. It didn't matter that, to analogize, he sat by his Coleman camp stove, cooking game and reading the latest copy of *Field and Stream* magazine with his rifle stashed in the gun rack in his old pick-up truck. No, he was secular; he had no interest or concern about covenant matters, about divine promises or divine privileges. That 'despised' (v. 34) is a strong verb. And there have always been Esaus who've said, 'No thanks, I really prefer the outer darkness.'

2

Ordinary People and the Kingdom of God
(Genesis 26:1-33)

I once wrote a commentary on the Book of Judges (Christian Focus, 2000) in which I devoted a whole chapter (well, three pages) to Shamgar (Judg. 3:31) simply because I thought Shamgar was too easily passed over; he deserved a chapter all to himself. Isaac is a bit like Shamgar. Isaac never gets anything all to himself—he appears in chapters 25 and 27, but other characters and matters tend to overshadow him. Pioneering Abraham, hairy Esau, and sly Jacob all eclipse him. Genesis 26 is the only chapter Isaac gets all to himself, but, alas, even here Esau gets his foot in the last two verses (vv. 34-35)! It's true that our whole section is dubbed the *toledoth* of Isaac (25:19) and so will focus on what *develops from* Isaac, but chapter 26 tells us a bit of Isaac himself.

We should note the *timing* of this episode. Right before our passage we have Jacob and Esau as grown men in the transfer-of-the-birthright segment (25:29-34). Right after our text, we meet with a forty-year-old Esau contracting dubious marriages (26:34-35). In between sits 26:1-33 in which, among other things, Isaac tries to pass off ravishing Rebekah as his sister. That means the episodes in 26:1-33 occurred sometime during the first twenty years of their marriage *before* they had any children (25:20-21, 26). Isaac's she's-my-sister routine would have never worked if there were a couple of urchins calling out, 'Mommy' (or even 'Daddy') around Rebekah's tent.[1] So 26:1-33 is something of a flashback to an earlier time and one wonders exactly why the writer so suddenly wrenches us back to an earlier time. Perhaps he felt the need to 're-set' the story and structure of the covenant before readers would meet the turbulence and mayhem over Jacob. And the account is constructed very carefully: a place or key term occurs at the beginning of each section and then again at the end of that section:

Vv. 1-6	Gerar … Gerar
Vv. 7-11	wife …wife
Vv. 12-22	land … land
Vv. 23-33	Beersheba … Beersheba

All through this passage Isaac walks in the shadow of Abraham – his problems and dilemmas are the same as Abraham faced.[2] But Isaac is no Abraham – nor does he need to be. When I was a lad, in pre-television days in our home, I would stand on late winter afternoons near the heat in our kitchen (while my mother worked on supper) and listen to a radio serial called 'Just Plain Bill.' And I suppose that may be how Isaac appears next to Abraham and Jacob. Just Plain Isaac. But the text is encouraging, for it tells us that *Yahweh is more than enough for everything His 'ordinary' people face.*

Notice, first, **that the problems are the same … and the promise is the same** (vv. 1-6). Another famine – like what

---

1. Cf. S. G. DeGraaf, *Promise and Deliverance*, 4 vols. (St. Catharines: Paideia, 1977), 1:178.

2. See John H. Sailhamer, *The Pentateuch as Narrative* (Grand Rapids: Zondervan, 1992), p. 186.

Abraham had faced (12:10). Of course, we don't know precise time periods in Genesis 12, but it seems like Abram no sooner begins his sojourn in the land of promise than he thinks he has to leave it for Egypt. And now Isaac faces the same problem. Isaac moved on to Gerar, probably about seventeen miles northwest of Beersheba, and, as Steinmann suggests, on the southwest edge of Canaan. In view of Yahweh's words in verse 2, Isaac may have intended to make Gerar a temporary stop on his way to Egypt. But Yahweh 'appeared' to him and nixed that plan.

Yahweh tells Isaac to 'sojourn in this land' (v. 3a), around Gerar, and then He fleshes out for him all the 'pieces' of the covenant promise. It's as if Yahweh says, 'Stay here and I will be for you all you need me to be.' In any case, Yahweh assures him of every component of that promise: (1) **presence** or protection ('I will be with you,' v. 3b); (2) **place** ('for to you and to your seed I will give all these lands,' vv. 3c, 4b); (3) **people** ('And I shall multiply your seed like the stars of the sky,' v. 4a); and (4) **program** ('And in your seed all the nations of the earth shall be blessed,' or, 'consider themselves blessed,' v. 4c). Elsewhere I have called this the 'quad promise,' because of the four elements that comprise it.[3] Sometimes the Lord may highlight one or two aspects of this promise, but here He presses home all four.

Might it be telling that the very first aspect of the promise Yahweh mentions is that of 'presence'? 'And I will be with you and will bless you' (v. 3a). Steinmann points out that 'this is the first time that God's promise to be with someone is recorded in Scripture.'[4] And 'ordinary' Isaac receives it. Whether famine or some other distress, is not this the assurance we covet most?

---

3. See my *The Word Became Fresh* (Ross-shire: Christian Focus, 2006), pp. 31-43.

4. Andrew E. Steinmann, *Genesis*, TOTC (London: Inter-Varsity, 2019), p. 256.

Another famine – the problems are the same as Abraham's; but the promise is the same as well.

There's something here, by way of footnote, that we shouldn't miss. Yahweh had referred in verse 5 to Abraham's comprehensive obedience. But after that the writer quite simply reports Isaac's obedience: 'So Isaac stayed in Gerar' (v. 6).

David Ellis tells of an unforgettable message he heard years ago at the old Glasgow Bible Training Institute. In what were literally his last days, Dr. Johnstone Jeffrey had been invited to address the students. He told them he simply wanted to read them his favorite Psalm, which was 139. When he finished it he seemed already exhausted. His message consisted of 'three halting sentences': 'Young people often have problems with guidance for the future.' Long, long pause. 'God will always give you enough light to take one more step.' Another long pause. Then: 'Take that step.' With that he sat down.[5] 'Sojourn in this land.' No prognosis about the famine, no long-term projections. 'And Isaac stayed in Gerar.' He took that step. The problems are the same, the promise is the same – and the obedience is the same.

The second segment of our text shows that **the peril is the same … and the protection is the same** (vv. 7-11). Rebekah was a 'looker' (last of v. 7), and a good-looking wife can be a problem. Men in Gerar had eyes. They asked Isaac about Rebekah. He's afraid the locals will 'take him out' over Rebekah if he admits she's his wife, so he tells them she's his sister. That may relieve his danger but increases hers. That was a workable ruse because at this time they had no children.

This was the same recourse Abraham had used in Egypt (12:11-15) and with, perhaps, a previous Abimelech (20:2).[6]

---

5. David W. Ellis, *Through All the Changing Scenes of Life* (Ross-shire: Christian Focus, 2020), pp. 191-92.

6. If 'Abimelech' is a dynastic name, we may have Abimelech I in Genesis 20 and Abimelech II in Genesis 26. If so, is Phicol, Abimelech's military aide

It was, overall, a failure to believe the protection-clause (12:3a) or the presence-clause (26:3) of Yahweh's promise. By implication it should teach us not to say, 'I won't repeat the mistakes of others.'

I've claimed that the 'protection is the same,' and that's true – sort of. That is, God did deliver Isaac and Rebekah in this mess. But He doesn't follow the same pattern as He did in delivering Abraham. He brought severe plagues on Pharaoh (12:17) and scared the liver out of Abimelech I with a death threat (20:3). But in Isaac's case God's deliverance was not so 'intrusive' but seems much more natural. One day Abimelech was peering down through the window and caught an eyeful (v. 8). It's a bit of a challenge to translate what he saw because of the word-play: the verb form following Isaac's name is from the same root as Isaac's name. So it could be, 'Laughter was laughing with Rebekah his wife.' The root carries the idea of joking or amusing oneself. Someone has suggested the colloquial 'horsing around,' which likely comes close, or, with the romantic tinge involved here, what some would call 'making out.' One can almost imagine Abimelech's shock: 'Look, Isaac, I have a sister – but I never kiss her like *that!*' So Isaac is exposed, rebuked, and protected (v. 11). But it all seemed to happen so naturally.

Though I'm sure I've alluded to it somewhere before, an anecdote about Charles Spurgeon comes to mind. Spurgeon

(21:22; 26:26), the same fellow in both cases, or might his be a 'family' name as well (see Steinmann, p. 261)? The years, however, between the Abimelech treaty of ch. 21 and that of ch. 26 are not as many as some commentators assume – remember ch. 26 takes place before Isaac and Rebekah have children, i.e., between Isaac's 40th and 60th years (25:20, 26). That there are three she's-my-sister episodes (chs. 12, 20, 26) in Genesis is not all that surprising. At least in Abraham's case, this sister-ruse was a matter of *operating policy* (see 20:13), so one would rather expect more than one occasion of this practice. For a recent attempt mostly to exonerate the patriarchs' deceptions, cf. Matthew Newkirk, 'Pimps or Protectors? A Re-examination of the Wife-Sister Deceptions,' *Journal of the Evangelical Theological Society*, 64 (2021): 45-57; in my view, there are too many debatable points to make his case stick.

was still a teenager when serving his first 'charge' in the village of Waterbeach. There was an old woman in that flock known for her abusive tongue. Charles had heard about her and one morning as he passed her house he experienced one of her tirades. She went on scolding him of multiple offenses. He smiled and replied, 'Yes, thank you; I'm quite well; I hope you are the same.' This brought on another nasty barrage. Smiling, Charles said, 'Yes, it does look rather as if it's going to rain; I think I had better be getting on.' The woman gave up. 'Bless the man, he's as deaf as a post; what is the use of storming at him?'[7] I fear I would have been more direct: 'Look, lady, if you don't like it, go help another church.' But sometimes the indirect is far more effective – and interesting. And God's protection operated overtly in Abraham's case (chs. 12, 20) but much more indirectly and 'naturally' in Isaac's – which is reason to praise Him for the delightful variety of His ways.

We shouldn't leave this segment without observing what a real place fear has in the lives of God's people. How very fragile we are. Children and teens have fears; all sorts of adults have fears. It's not that we can never tremble, but we must pray to be faith-*full* in our fears.

Third, the story shows that **the pressures are the same … and the provision is the same** (vv. 12-22). Difficulties arose, well, because Yahweh blessed him (v. 12b). He was ludicrously successful in farming (v. 12a) and his wealth markedly increased in both livestock and employees (vv. 13-14). The locals envied him and so Abimelech & Co. ordered Isaac to leave their turf – having someone so close with such power and weight was apparently not in the Philistines' 'best interests' (v. 16). Then the troubles started over water rights. This had become a problem for Abram and Lot in chapter 13, but it was

---

7. Lewis Drummond, *Spurgeon: Prince of Preachers* (Grand Rapids: Kregel, 1992), p. 166.

solved by an amicable separation, though Abraham had had his own gripes about the problem with Abimelech (21:25).

The water problem doubtless had been aggravated by the Philistines. The ESV is probably right in seeing verse 15 as a parenthetical note, a sort of for-your-information clue. The local Philistines may have been spiteful and envious of Abraham as well – in any case, they filled up his wells with dirt. In the Old Testament Philistines are never noted for their brilliance (well, read Judges 14–16 and 1 Samuel 4–6 for a start).[8] You may say that that sounds like an ethnic slur, and it is. Well-deserved. After all, if it's true that 'Cretans are always liars, evil brutes, lazy gluttons' (Titus 1:12-13a, NIV), why not say so?

But this aggravates Isaac's problem. Where to get water for his burgeoning livestock? One can't simply order 'Water on Wheels' from the volunteers at the Gerar Community Center. No, this causes major distress. Especially when Isaac's men (re-?) dig wells and then had the locals contest Isaac's rights to that water (vv. 19-21). So those wells were named Contention and Hostility. Isaac moved still further away; they dug again; no disputes; name of well – Rehoboth ('spaces'). 'Yahweh has made space for us' (v. 22).

Rehoboth – that's how Isaac would spell relief. It's interesting, isn't it, how a mere name can conjure up a whole memory of either distress or deliverance? Mention 'Chancellorsville' to a southerner in my country (who has a tidbit of historical knowledge) and it would bring to mind 1863 and the tragic loss of General Stonewall Jackson to the Confederacy. Mention 'Dunkirk' to folks in the UK and the whole memory of the tension and deliverance of 1940 comes flooding in. And there are texts that pick up this 'space' or

---

8. Cf. my *Judges: Such a Great Salvation* (Ross-shire: Christian Focus, 2000), pp. 175-79.

'making room' idea in 'Rehoboth.' Think of Psalm 4:1, 'In (my) distress you have made space for me,' or Psalm 31:8, 'You … have set my feet in a spacious place' (NIV). Has the Lord given you some 'Rehoboths' as well? It might be well to go back over your biography, lest you have forgotten.

Finally, in verses 23-33, we find that **the place is the same …and the peace is the same.** Now Isaac goes to Beersheba, some twenty-five miles southwest of Hebron. This was where Abimelech I and Abraham had met and concluded a covenant (21:22-34). Now Isaac would do the same with his Abimelech counterpart.

But there's a 'peace' here before the formal peace from the conclusion of the Abimelech covenant. Note that Yahweh appeared to Isaac with His night-time assurance as soon as Isaac arrived (v. 24). Then verse 25 tells us: 'So he built there an altar and called on the name of Yahweh, and he pitched tent there, and Isaac's servants dug a well there.' Interesting that 'there' is used three times in that verse. One could say that this in itself is a picture of peace. Note the components: altar, tent, and well, implying worship, shelter, provision. Enough hopefully to make one content.

But then there is the peace that comes via the covenant (vv. 26-33). Isaac berates Abimelech & Co. He asks them why they are 'kissing up' over a non-aggression pact now when they had kicked him out of Gerar before (v. 27). Their response essentially is that they have no choice since Yahweh has obviously made Isaac's clan so successful and strong (vv. 28-29). It all brings to mind Proverbs 16:7, 'When the ways of a man please Yahweh, he makes even his enemies to be at peace with him.' Sometimes the Lord does that for you – He gives you peaceful relations or at least the respect of pagans; they may be repulsed by your faith, abominate your principles, and repudiate your lifestyle, and yet they regard you with favor nonetheless.

Let me add a footnote to this 'place-peace' section here in verses 23-33 – and do it by the back door. British historian Martin Gilbert once told of his research on Churchill's life. He said he started with fifteen tons of his letters and papers. He sifted through everything; he said he even read Sir Winston's laundry lists. Of what use could those be? Well, once Gilbert found a laundry list from a Beirut hotel. He had not known Churchill had been in Beirut. From the date on that laundry list Gilbert discovered a 1934 journey Churchill made to the Middle East that was not in the history books.[9] It was a mere hint, a date on a laundry list, that led to this discovery.

It seems to me that Abimelech and Isaac's covenant pow-wow has something of this character – a pointer to something much more significant. Isn't it, in one sense, a sample of 'all the families of the earth' being blessed in Abraham's seed (12:3) – already in the Book of Genesis? Like a mere date on a laundry list, does this point to far more? Something like Psalm 86:9 ('All nations which you have made will come and worship before you, O Lord, and will glorify your name'; see also Ps. 138:4-5)? I'm not arguing that this is a conversion experience for Abimelech, but only that in being compelled to seek out one obviously blessed by Yahweh, one might see a hint of the saving influx of Isaiah 2:2-3.

Isaac is not Abraham, but the promise, protection, provision, and peace he received is the same as Abraham enjoyed. All that God gave to Abraham He gives to Isaac. God's gifts are not determined by your prominence.

---

9. In Brian Lamb, ed., *Booknotes* (New York: Random House, 1997), pp. 57-58.

3

THE PROMISE OF GOD
AND FOUR SINNERS
(Genesis 26:34–28:9)

In the 1860s in Virginia there was an area called 'The Wilderness.' It began about eight to nine miles west of Fredericksburg and went on for some fifteen miles. The Wilderness consisted of second-growth forest, with a tangle of saplings and dense undergrowth, briars and brush. No problem – unless trying to fight a battle there as in my country's 'Civil War.' Then the woods became smoke-filled, units would lose direction and go blundering the wrong way, 'friendly' troops would fire on their own men. One usually couldn't see the enemy, could only shoot back at the bursts of flame one saw; shells would set underbrush on fire, much to the terror of the helpless wounded. No one could conduct the semblance of a cohesive battle on such turf. Something like the account we face, especially in chapter 27. One wonders how it is possible for God to work in such a chaotic mess.

But if the story is chaotic, the text is not. Our present section, 26:34–28:9, shows every evidence of careful planning. I would map out the text like this:

Esau marries, 26:34-35
 Isaac orders Esau, 27:1-4
  Rebekah directs Jacob, 27:5-17
   Jacob deceives Isaac, 27:18-25
    Jacob blessed, 27:26-29
   Isaac discovers deception, 27:30-33
    Esau 'deprived,' 27:34-40
  Rebekah directs Jacob, 27:41-46
 Isaac orders Jacob, 28:1-5
Esau marries, 28:6-9

I think this fairly represents the movement of our passage, though caution is always due, for it is easy to be over-enthusiastic about 'seeing' literary patterns. But when I see such careful packaging, I am always prone to think of it as coming from an original writer rather than being the final product of a committee of contributors of various traditions over hundreds of years. Old Testament critics who prefer to chunk up the Pentateuch into various documents or strata of tradition, with redactors here and redactors there, will vigorously object, but carefully structured pieces like this imply that much of their furrow-browed work is useless.[1]

We must, however, focus on the 'teaching points' of this segment, so let us notice the 'Esau' brackets (26:34-35 and 28:6-9) which suggest **the sad indifference to covenant life.**

These marriage notices seem to pick up the note of Esau's indifference from 25:34. The writer is very clear that Esau did not give a rip about the birthright. He does not scourge Jacob for driving a hard bargain – rather, he says, Esau could care less about the birthright. Apparently, the same nonchalance guided his domestic concerns – he marries two Hittite women

---

1. Some scholars see an overall literary pattern (chiasmus) for all of the Jacob narrative. I am not convinced of this, but see, e.g., G. J. Wenham, *Genesis 16–50*, WBC (Dallas: Word, 1994), pp. 168-70, and Kenneth A. Mathews, *Genesis 11:27–50:26*, NAC (Nashville: Broadman & Holman, 2005), pp. 376-79.

(26:34). Who knows precisely *how* they made things bitter for Esau's parents, but they did (v. 35).

Esau's self-directed pattern stands in sharp contrast to the strenuous efforts of Abraham to obtain a suitable wife for Isaac in chapter 24. His burning concern was that his servant *not* take a wife for Isaac from the pool of the local Canaanite girls (24:3). And it took all of sixty-seven verses to get it right! But covenant distinctiveness is of no concern to Esau. Even when he realized what a pain his wives were to Isaac, he didn't really help matters by marrying a daughter of Ishmael (28:8-9), adding still another wife, a kind of un-correcting correction. 'To take a third wife, even though an Ishmaelite was better than a Hittite, was hardly the way back to blessing.'[2]

Sometimes it's easy to read attitudes and perspectives off of actions. George Thomas was a general in the War Between the States – he fought for the north. That was a bit of a problem because he himself was from the south, Virginia. When the war broke out, he had to decide, like many in the military, where and whom he would serve. He felt his allegiance was owed to the original US government and so he became part of the Federal army. But back at the old home place in Virginia, his two unmarried sisters turned his picture to the wall.[3] No doubt about their attitude!

Sometimes it's not that overt but nevertheless clear. It's not that Esau was brandishing the Humanist Manifesto or

---

2. Derek Kidner, *Genesis* (London: Tyndale, 1967), p. 157. The lists of Esau's wives here in 26:34 and 28:9 and then in 36:2-3 is as yet an insoluble conundrum. It could well be that by chapter 36 time, Judith (26:34a) had died and that Oholibamah (36:2) was an additional wife taken after those of chs. 26 and 28. But how the Basemath of 26:34 and Adah in 36:2 could be the same (both 'the daughter of Elon the Hittite') or how Mahalath of 28:9 could be the same as Basemath of 36:3 (both daughter of Ishmael, sister of Nebaioth) is more than unclear.

3. Benson Bobrick, *Master of War* (New York: Simon and Schuster, 2009), pp. 37, 65.

some secularist creed. It's simply how and whom he married – that said a lot. And still does. If you want to know where the priorities of a professing Christian man or woman really lie, watch the decision they make when selecting a mate. It will tell you whether Bible commandments matter to them, whether they care about influences on any future family, whether they think there is a proper distinction between the church and the world. Or whether, sadly, none of that really matters.

Secondly, chapter 27 depicts **the pervasive perversity of covenant people.** Here is where 'the promise of God and four sinners' comes into play. There are two items we must remember when considering this story in chapter 27. One is Yahweh's clear word to Rebekah, 'The older will serve the younger' (25:23). We assume, but rightly assume, that Rebekah made known this revelation to Isaac. It would be unthinkable that she would or could keep this as a private secret. So Isaac knew of Yahweh's plan. A second item, not as dominant perhaps but which ought to be noted: Esau's oath in 25:33. Esau had already gone on oath to Jacob, bartering away his precedence to Jacob. Now … what we meet in chapter 27 is the saga of God's Word and the conspiracy against it, or, for and against it. We'll take each of the players in turn.

Here's Isaac (vv. 1-4). He's always favored Esau (25:28) and now he proposes they have a fine ceremonial affair. Esau should hunt game, prepare it in the tasty fashion Isaac loves, he will eat it and give the blessing to Esau. Isaac can't see (perhaps his cataracts were severe) but he still lived by his senses: taste (v. 4), touch (vv. 11, 16, 22-23), smell (v. 27), and hearing (v. 22). But he's a stubborn old coot. Without doubt he knew the word God had spoken (25:23) and yet he flies in the face of it (v. 4). Here is opposition to the expressed Word of God. Who knows? Perhaps he had rationalized that he could still direct covenant affairs his way. Isaac places *palate over promise.* He is the patron saint of all who say, 'I don't really care what the Word of God says, I will follow my own feelings.'

Isaac's program stirs Rebekah into motion (vv. 5-10). We can summarize Rebekah's approach as *action eclipses faith*. Not to be unkind, but she is an idolatrous activist. She cannot wait and let God sort things out – she must intervene and put things right. 'We have to fix this – and fast.' Looking at verses 7-9, one wonders if Rebekah didn't rankle at how Isaac drooled over Esau's barbecue. She could stir up the same sort of stuff with goat meat, and Isaac couldn't tell the difference. You just needed to know how to season it. Rebekah is the patron saint of all who serve a 'helpless' god, who has no hands but our hands and no resources but our schemes. She does not simply broach the promise issue with Isaac (she avoids 'confrontation'?) and leave it in Yahweh's hands. Rather, she seeks to manipulate and, well, deceive. God is a great promiser, but we cannot trust Him to care for and protect His own promise. We think we must 'help God out' because He is not adequate to care for His own cause.

Jacob's role requires little comment (vv. 11-12, 18-19, 24). But verses 11-12 are especially revealing. After hearing Rebekah's plan, he does not exclaim, 'Mother, I'm shocked over your ethics!' No, he does not say the plan is wicked but that it's unworkable. Jacob operates on the principle of *pragmatism over righteousness*. If God's promise is right, it should be fulfilled in a right way – but not for Jacob. He is not above straight-out lying (vv. 19, 24), as long as it seems safe.

Then we meet Esau's reaction, especially in verses 34, 36, and 38. Esau's emotional meltdown here needs to be viewed in light of 25:29-34. Probably in forfeiting the birthright, Esau forfeited the right to the blessing, but in any event it is crucial to hold to the writer's judgment in 25:34 that Esau *despised* the birthright. And he definitely and clearly submitted it to Jacob (25:33). When he complains that Jacob 'took away my birthright' (v. 36), he is as big a liar as Jacob. He is a belly-aching, whining hypocrite. *Indifference in spite of emotion* sums up Esau's stance. Don't let his tears impress you too much.

Where does this leave us? With four sinners and all of them in the wrong, whether they were for or against the promise. Isaac's rebellion, Rebekah and Jacob's deception, and Esau's blubbering paint a collage of perversity. Other narratives in Genesis raise the same point as this one, but chapter 27 certainly raises it: How can all the families of the ground be blessed (12:3) through a people like this? How can Yahweh dream of using such scurvy characters in any way to His glory? Contemporary covenant people should not be tempted into thinking they belong to a higher class, for the text is telling us that the kingdom of God does not come because the church is so faithful.

Finally, then, the text wants to stress **the victorious sovereignty of the covenant God.** At the end of it all, Yahweh's decree ('the older will serve the younger,' 25:23) comes to pass in spite of direct opposition and devious assistance. *Yahweh's will is going to triumph in spite of all efforts to sabotage it –* in spite of the network of 'free' and sinful wills opposing or 'aiding' His decision. God brings His Word to pass, if not through man's consent, then in spite of his resistance; if not through man's cooperation, then through and over his rebellion. Yahweh has such marvelous ways of overcoming all hindrances in order to effect His designs.

This is not only the case in 'negative' situations, like that in our text, but in more 'positive' ones in which He uses such unlikely circumstances to fulfill His will. For example, during the time of Charles Spurgeon's ministry in nineteenth-century England, a certain evangelist was asked to go to a 'public house' in Nottingham and see the landlord's wife. She was dying. The evangelist reported that he found her rejoicing in

Christ as her Savior. The evangelist asked her how she had found the Lord. 'Reading that,' she answered, handing him a torn piece of paper. He looked at it and saw that it was part of an American newspaper containing an extract of one of Spurgeon's sermons. That extract had led to her conversion. He asked where she had gotten the newspaper. It was wrapped around a package that was sent to her from Australia! So, do the math: A sermon, preached in London, conveyed to America, an extract re-printed in an American newspaper, that paper sent to Australia, part torn off (accidentally?!) for the package being sent to Nottingham, and, after all the twists and turns, bringing the word of grace to that wife of a pub keeper.[4]

There is just such a persistence like that in God's ways, whether overcoming human messes, like in our text, or in turning unlikely circumstances into His instruments. I call this the 'stubbornness' of God. You won't find 'stubbornness' listed as an attribute of God in any systematic theology book. But I think it should be counted as one. This divine stubbornness should be of immense comfort to us – it tells us among other things that nothing, no human rebellion, no human stupidity can stop Yahweh's kingdom plan. God is so stubborn that He will make sure Jesus reigns over all the earth.

---

4. Lewis Drummond, *Spurgeon: Prince of Preachers* (Grand Rapids: Kregel, 1992), p. 326.

4

GRACE THAT IS GREATER THAN ALL OUR BUNGLING
(Genesis 28:10-22)

Former President Theodore Roosevelt wrote to his son Quentin, who was overseas, serving during the first World War. Quentin was not married but had an 'intended,' Flora Whitney. Both his parents liked her very much. But Quentin rarely wrote Flora. Letters weren't everything but a lack of them could kill a relationship. So 'Teddy' wrote Quentin and told him:

> If you want to lose her, continue to be an infrequent correspondent. If, however, you wish to keep her, write her letters – interesting letters, and love letters – at least three times a week. Write no matter how tired you are ... Write enough letters to allow for half being lost.[1]

Quentin responded properly. But Teddy felt he had to intervene to get matters on track.

As we've seen, Rebekah is an 'intervener', seeking to set things to rights, as least as she saw matters. Now she's at it

---

1. H. W. Brands, *T. R.: The Last Romantic* (New York: Basic Books, 1997), p. 791.

again in 27:41-45 and 27:46–28:5. There is a need for damage control. Esau plans to wipe out Jacob, so Rebekah tells Jacob he must go to Haran to her brother's household until Esau's anger cools – 'and,' as she says, 'he forgets what you have done to him' (v. 45). A bit naïve? Esau will *forget* that? But her real intervention involves Isaac. How to get that sluggish patriarch to use his authority in this matter? She uses a true situation as her 'cover,' so that Isaac will order Jacob to leave. She rehearses to Isaac a probably oft-repeated complaint: the misery of her life due to Esau's pagan wives (v. 46). 'I loathe my life because of the Hittite women.' It'll be ultimate disaster, Isaac, if Jacob marries one of them. Is that what you want, Isaac? Do you realize you need to *do* something about all this? So Isaac did, and Jacob was off to northwest Mesopotamia to fish for a wife among Rebekah's family (28:1-5).

'Jacob went out from Beersheba and went to Haran' (v. 10). Sometimes biblical journeys are that 'short' – no details, just a summary statement (cf. 29:1; 37:14b; 42:3; 43:15b), even though all sorts of interesting events may have occurred on the journey. In the present case, however, the text 'stops' to report a most momentous encounter. Since Jacob is in the area of Bethel, he had gone some fifty-five miles from Beersheba and this was probably about his third night on the road.[2] I think grace is the major theme of this episode – perhaps we could call it 'the grace of God in the "house of God"' [= Bethel].

First off, the text shows that **grace surprises** (vv. 11-13a). In his travel Jacob happens on to a particular place (lit., 'the place,' dubbed such three times in v. 11). As he sleeps that night he dreams, and his dream is full of surprises. Three times (vv. 12-13a) we meet with the form *wehinneh*, which has traditionally been anglicized as 'And behold.' *Hinneh*

---

2. John H. Walton, in ZIBBC, 1:106.

[sounds like: hin-nay] is a particle that indicates something is more or less startling. Sometimes one can capture the sense by translating 'Why,' as an exclamation:

> And he dreamed,
> and, why! – a stairway situated on earth
> with its top reaching into the sky,
> and, why! – angels of God going up
> and coming down on it,
> and, why! – Yahweh standing over him (vv. 12-13a).[3]

Jacob hardly surmised this would occur. He didn't arrive thinking, 'You know, I'll probably dream tonight and Yahweh will appear and speak to me.' This was a complete surprise. Something like what Spurgeon received when he'd written an article and made an off-hand remark about the need for a facility where some of London's neglected street orphans could be cared for. He received a note from a Mrs. Hillyard, widow of a wealthy Church of England clergyman, pledging 20,000 pounds for the work. Spurgeon was agog, went with one of his men to visit her and said they'd come to thank her for the 200 pounds she'd offered. She exclaimed, 'Did I write 200? I meant 20,000.' Spurgeon thought there may have been one or two too many zeroes![4] Utter surprise.

That is the mood of this text. Oh, we can go on and on about the 'stairway' and how it might be related to Mesopotamian ziggurats or how we might compare it to the tower of Babel in chapter 11. But angels are there; Yahweh is there. There's a certain ease about it all, as if Yahweh were saying to Jacob, 'It's not hard for me to get to you.' The stairway did not suggest

---

3. Translations differ over whether Yahweh stands 'above it' (the stairway) or 'beside him' (Jacob; or, 'over him'). I prefer the latter; see V. P. Hamilton, *The Book of Genesis: Chapters 18–50*, NICOT (Grand Rapids: Eerdmans, 1995), pp. 240-41.

4. Lewis Drummond, *Spurgeon: Prince of Preachers* (Grand Rapids: Kregel, 1992), pp. 420-21.

Jacob's access to God but God's to Jacob – He could 'get to' him anytime, anywhere.

Probably none of us have ever slept and dreamed at Bethel but can still remember being surprised by grace. There was the mess you had made, the relationship ruined, the habit that was destroying you – or maybe it was the loss of a job or major surgery; you had no idea heaven could take an interest in you. And God showed up. It may be without the stairway and the angels but grace still surprises.

Secondly, looking at the promise in verses 13b-15 and viewing it contextually, we can say that **grace offends**. Yahweh re-affirms His covenant commitment to Jacob, in terms very much like His assurance to Abraham in 12:1-3 and to Isaac in 26:3-4. But doesn't this bother you, upset and anger you? Isn't there something terribly 'wrong' in this? After all, we've just come out of chapter 27, where Jacob was only one of four culprits but was certainly one of them. One who had no ethics (27:11-12), one who could speak bald-faced lies at the drop of a hat (27:19, 24). And here is Yahweh speaking extended assurances to Jacob! If you were God, you would have no truck with this lying, scheming, low-down, self-serving, sneaky mama's boy. There's something about grace that makes us angry.

Henry Gerecke was a US Army chaplain who was asked to serve among the Nazis on trial at Nuremberg in 1946. He spoke German which was one 'plus' in a difficult ministry. He met with these men who would be condemned to death or marooned in prison; he questioned, counseled, prayed. He began 'chapel services.' Several of the men seemed genuinely repentant. Gerecke was no softee. He'd had much experience dealing with criminal types. Some of those he examined he admitted to the Lord's supper. Near Christmas of 1945 Gerecke noted what looked like genuine change in the attitudes of Fritzsche, Schirach, and a couple of others. Even the arrogant and obnoxious Ribbentrop seemed to have cast himself upon Christ. Gerecke's duties as an army chaplain ended in July 1950, and he continued in ministry until his death in 1961. After his death his oldest son found a thick file of letters stashed in a secret compartment of his father's desk. They had been sent from all over the United States. They called Gerecke a 'Jew-hater,' a 'Nazi-lover,' and said he should have been hanged at Nuremberg with the rest of them. All the letters were written in the most hateful language imaginable.[5] Why such venom, why so vicious? That's what grace does – it offends. Those who have little knowledge of themselves implicitly sense that grace is something that should not be.

However, we are all 'Jacobs.' Let's not even think of actions, but if you have any knowledge of your motives and imaginations and thoughts and desires, how can you not see that you have no hope apart from this offensive, shouldn't-be-stuff called grace? In grace God tramples on all our snooty ideas of propriety. If grace galls you, you are still a stranger to it.

Third, we see that **grace overflows** (vv. 13b-15). As noted above, Jacob receives Yahweh's promise in all its full provision, nothing is held back; the promise is as extensive as that given Abraham and Isaac (12:1-3; 26:3-5), all four 'legs' of it:

Place: '...the land on which you are lying, to you I will give it and to your seed' (v. 13b).

People: 'And your seed shall be like the dust of the earth and shall break forth to the west and east and north and south' (v. 14a).

Program: 'And all the families of the ground shall be blessed in you—and in your seed' (v. 14b).

Presence/protection: 'And see, I am with you, and shall keep you wherever you go ...' (v. 15).

---

5. Don Stephens, *War and Grace* (Darlington: Evangelical Press, 2005), pp. 253-71.

And yet there's a problem in this lavishness; the promise seems to promise too much. Once more, we are eyeball-to-eyeball with the *unlikelihood* of it all. Well, think of the 'place.' Yahweh says He will give Jacob the land 'on which you are lying' – but Jacob is in the process of *leaving* that land. Think too of the 'people'-aspect: his seed, Yahweh says, will be like the dust of the earth, but he doesn't even have a wife, let alone children. It hardly seems we can give Yahweh's promise five stars for relevance.

Yet there is one provision of this promise that had immediate application to Jacob's circumstances. In early 1865 Joshua Speed came to visit his friend, President Lincoln, in the White House. Lincoln had to finish up with his time for visitors and so Speed waited for Lincoln to finish with that chore. Lincoln's last two visitors were two women, one the mother, the other the wife, of a man arrested for resisting the draft. Lincoln granted their petition and spared the son and husband. Then he wearily pulled up a chair to visit with Speed. His friend scolded Lincoln for exhausting himself and spending his time on petitioners like the last two women. 'How much you are mistaken,' Lincoln replied; 'I have made two people happy today.'[6] Lincoln was worn down with incessant claims on his time and with all the other concerns near the close of the Civil War, but there was something he had accomplished 'today.'

That is what Yahweh does in this promise. No matter how far off some promise provisions may be, no matter how unlikely they presently appear, no matter that we can't project how Yahweh will ever bring them to pass, nevertheless Yahweh has something for Jacob's 'today' – 'I am with you, and I shall keep you wherever you go' (v. 15). This assurance is not for down the road but for right now. What this must have meant to the ears of an exile,

---

6. David Herbert Donald, *'We Are Lincoln Men'* (New York: Simon & Schuster, 2003), p. 64.

who was without home, without family, without clarity on what would come next! But since Yahweh is 'with' him, he has all he needs in 'the now.' And do not 'New Testament Christians' find the same? We haven't yet seen the full 'immeasurable riches of his grace' (Eph. 2:7) and yet how often have we said, with Paul, 'But the Lord stood by me and gave me strength' (2 Tim. 4:17)?

Finally, from Jacob's responses it's clear the **grace impresses** (vv. 16-22). You first see the impact of grace in Jacob's *surprise* (v. 16). 'Surely Yahweh is in this place, and I, I did not know it.' Unlike John, who was 'in the Spirit on the Lord's Day' (Rev. 1:10), Jacob was not expecting Yahweh's coming to him. Matthew Henry was right: 'We sometimes meet with God where we little thought of meeting with him,' and then he adds, 'No place excludes divine visits.'[7] That may prove unnerving (as it seemed to do with Jacob), but a little thought suggests how glorious it is.

Then grace leaves its mark in *fear*: 'So he was afraid and said, "How fearful this place is! This is nothing but the house of God, this is the gate to heaven"' (v. 17). When you find yourself in Yahweh's presence you do not become casual and informal. And there is nothing incompatible between grace and trembling. Fear can be the evidence that grace has hit its target. Then grace also brings *commitment* (vv. 18-22). Here Jacob's response begins by marking out the place with a pillar and calling the place 'the house of God,' Bethel (vv. 18-19). And then he goes on to express his commitment in a vow (vv. 20-22).

We need to turn aside to deal with the translation of Jacob's vow. Most English translations carry the 'if'-clauses through the first of verse 21, and understand the second clause of verse 21 as the beginning of the 'then'-conclusion (apodosis). However, as Hamilton points out, the pattern of the grammar

---

7. *Matthew Henry's Commentary on the Whole Bible*, 6 vols. (New York: Revell, n.d.), 1:173.

makes it more likely that verse 22 begins the 'then'-clause.[8] So it would read like this:

> If God will be with me
> and shall keep me in this way I'm going,
> and shall give me bread to eat and clothing to wear,
> and I shall return safely to my father's house,
> and Yahweh shall be my God,
> then this stone which I have set up as a pillar
>   will be the house of God,
> and as for all that you give me,
>   I will give the tenth to you.

Jacob is not bargaining with God but vowing to God. He is responding to what Yahweh had promised in verses 13-15, as if to say, 'If Yahweh does all this for me, then I will respond in worship (22a) and giving (22b), I will establish worship here at "Bethel" and I will give a tenth to Yahweh.' The 'worship' portion was not fulfilled until 35:1-7.

The keynote of the section is that grace leaves its mark – in surprise, fear, and commitment; it changes us. Warren Wiersbe has told of Executive Committee meetings at Moody Church. Apparently, they could often generate conflict and discord. He says that George Sweeting once came to the Monday night Executive Committee meeting carrying a machete one of the church's missionaries had given him. He laid it on the conference table and said with a smile, 'Now, men, there'll be no trouble tonight!'[9] *That* would make a profound impression! That is what 'Bethel' did for Jacob. Only we must not think that it brought about some form of comprehensive sanctification. God had more work to do with Jacob. But 'Bethel' left its mark.

---

8. For the argument, both grammatical and theological, see Hamilton, p. 248.

9. Warren W. Wiersbe, *Be Myself* (Wheaton, IL: Victor, 1994), pp. 232-33.

5

A Bit of Glad, Bad, and Sad
(Genesis 29:1-30)

Norman Rockwell depicted a maybe six-year-old boy sitting on a stool at the counter in a 1950s-type diner with a bundle of clothes (or what-not) tied to a stick on the floor beneath the stool. A policeman sits on the stool next to the lad, giving him a kind of where-do-you-think-you're-going look. It's called 'The Runaway,' though of course he's going to be taken right back home. In this passage Jacob is the runaway but there's no way he can go back home. He had to get out and stay away since Esau was bent on making Jacob disposable. But the nice thing about biblical journeys is that many of them take no time at all. 'Jacob picked up his feet and went to the land of the people of the East' (v. 1, Wenham). One verse and we're 550 miles away![1] Now the tricky part is that God is never mentioned in this passage; so how do we know what He is doing, how He assesses matters, or what we are to infer about the teaching of the text? When a text is 'godless' in this sense, interpretation becomes more challenging. However, I think the text wants to underscore three matters.

---

1. IVPBBC, p. 60.

First, the text wants us to think about **providence** (vv. 1-14). Jacob comes upon some shepherds and begins asking questions (vv. 4-6): Where are they from? Do they know Laban? Is he well? One wonders if Jacob was normally like contemporary males. We men like to find people and places *without* asking questions. But Jacob didn't have MapQuest or iPhone or even Rand McNally and so he had to ask. He was in the right area. And yet at the same time he ran into a cultural bugaboo. And he couldn't help bringing it up (v. 7) – why were these fellows lounging around? They should water the sheep and go pasture them. It really bothered Jacob to see this. It reminds me of being in someone's house for a meal and dessert time comes round. The dessert is one to which ice cream is customarily added. But after the dessert is served, I sometimes note that the host or hostess just leaves the ice cream package out on the table or counter. That always bothers me. It's going to melt. It needs to be put back in the freezer. Why do they let it sit there? So Jacob comes face up with this, to him, nonsensical local custom. But the laconic response is that the shepherds have to wait until all the flocks are there and then, together, they move the stone on the well and water the flocks. 'That's just the way we do it here.'

Rachel arrives with part of Laban's flock, and Jacob plays macho-man, moves the stone from the well by himself and waters Rachel's sheep (v. 10). After that he discloses himself to her (vv. 11-12) and eventually to Laban (vv. 13-14). You can imagine the talk at the local convenience store that evening: 'That boy can sure handle big stones, I want ya to know.'

That is the story, and we have to ask about its significance. Jacob came right where he needed to be (v. 4), to track down the people he needed to find (v. 5), and, of all things, he simply bumps into the very household he was looking for (v. 6). Is that not the kind providence of God? Unlike the episode in Genesis 24, this one is not saturated with thanksgiving and praise. Did Jacob not 'see' God's providence here? Not as dramatic perhaps as that in chapter 24 – was it largely ignored? A safe journey of hundreds of miles, a successful destination – does Jacob take it as a matter of course? Maybe it seems so, well, natural, like Ruth's ending up in Boaz's barley field (Ruth 2:3) or the anonymous disciple who asked Elisha to go along on the dormitory construction venture (2 Kings 6:3).

In 1861 the War Between the States erupted in my country when South Carolina forces bombarded the northern troops holding Fort Sumter. In the barrage between attackers and defenders about 4,000 shells were fired, without killing anyone on either side.[2] Obviously, they weren't *trying* for a safety record! But I wonder if anyone pondered that? I wonder if anyone thought to give thanks? My wife just returned from the grocery store a few minutes ago. It may be a round trip of ten miles – in the rain today. She came back safely, and we tend to expect that, I suppose. But it's really a gift. God has been quietly good, again. Just because God does not announce His providence with the blare of trumpets is no reason for us not to acknowledge it, whether in Haran or Dundee.

Discipline is the second matter our text underscores (vv. 15-27). However we take verse 15 (there seems to be some debate), Laban seems willing to pay Jacob wages for his work. At this point the narrative provides some parenthetical information about Laban's daughters (vv. 16-17). Leah is the older with eyes, according to some translations, that are 'weak.' But the word can mean 'soft' or 'tender.' Leah may have beautiful eyes, but Rachel is a real catch, both in face and figure (17b). Jacob is captivated by Rachel and strikes a deal with Laban – seven years of work for the right to marry Rachel (vv. 18-20). Jacob had no bride price to offer and so had to

---

2. Bruce Catton, *The Coming Fury* (Garden City, NY: Doubleday, 1961), p. 324. An accident afterwards took some lives, but the mutual bombardment did not.

give 'sweat equity.' But the story goes into 'fast forward,' and within one verse (20) we are seven years along. That's when the fiasco heats up.

Jacob demanded his bride and Laban put on a marriage feast (vv. 21-22). 'Shifty' may have been Laban's middle name: he took Leah and brought her to Jacob, who spent the night with her, only to get the shocker of his life in the morning – 'Oh, no! It was Leah!' (v. 25a). The story is not going to fill in all the details. For Laban's scheme to work we must understand that Leah was veiled. When Laban put on the feast it was called a *mishteh,* a drinking feast. So, among other things, Jacob was likely a bit inebriated, only to become terribly sober in the morning. He simply blew his stack at Laban and irony almost drips off the page when he exclaims, 'Why have you deceived me?' (v. 25b). That's an intriguing concept. But Laban was ready with an 'explanation.' It's as if he says, 'Oh, Jacob, I may have neglected to tell you, but the cultural convention here is that the younger sister cannot be married before the older' (cf. v. 26). Perhaps Laban went on rather breezily, 'But, no worries! Finish the wedding week, and I'll let you have your Rachel. Of course, you'll owe me another seven years!' (v. 27). Laban has out-jacobed Jacob. The deceiver (chapter 27) has been deceived.

Some years back someone sent in an anecdote to *Leadership* magazine about Sir Robert Watson Watt, who had invented radar. Watt was arrested in Canada for speeding – he'd been caught in a radar trap. To commemorate, I suppose, he penned a poem:

> Pity Sir Robert Watson Watt,
> strange target of his radar plot,
> and this, with others, I could mention,
> a victim of his own invention.

Sir Robert clearly got the point, but one can't tell from the text whether Jacob did. The irony of it all brings to mind Adoni-bezek. The men of Judah caught him, hacked off his thumbs and big toes, which led him to confess: 'Seventy kings with their thumbs and their big toes hacked off used to pick up scraps under my table – as I have done, so God has repaid me' (Judg. 1:7).

We, however, should get the point. This passage never mentions God but clearly He is at work. There *is* a discipline He may bring, and sometimes a rough one. And we are called not to 'take lightly' the discipline of the Lord (cf. Heb. 12:5). Jacob's response should have been: 'God is putting me into His "school", trying to pound some sense into my head.'

The third note in our passage is **sadness** (vv. 28-30). So Jacob gets his Rachel and works another seven years. The 'sadness' appears in verse 30, where most versions translate 'he loved Rachel more than Leah.' But this may be too mild. The preposition here is probably one of *exclusion* rather than comparison. Translate, then: 'he loved Rachel rather than Leah.'[3] Jacob did not love Leah at all.[4]

Leah cuts a tragic figure. She was used by her father in his scheme to deceive Jacob. There's no indication that that was her idea. She is ignored (mostly) by her husband, and her children were less favored (see later). She seemed to be always used, never loved, seldom wanted – and, finally, buried (cf. 49:31). Sometimes folks criticize the Old Testament for

3. See John D. Currid, *A Study Commentary on Genesis*, 2 vols. (Darlington: Evangelical Press, 2003), 2:84; see also Bruce K. Waltke and M. O'Connor, *An Introduction to Biblical Hebrew Syntax* (Winona Lake, IN: Eisenbrauns, 1990), p. 265.

4. The story is clear that Jacob married sisters and had them as wives at the same time. This shows that this story is old, because simultaneous marriage to sisters was later illegal and forbidden in the law of God (Lev. 18:18). But this also shows that this story is *true*, for it wasn't 're-written' or 'edited' or 'cleaned up' to make it fit later stipulations. Israel doesn't try to sanitize the stories of her forefathers.

not overtly condemning polygamy. But it does it subversively instead. The Bible doesn't have to stop and moralize on the matter but only to describe what it's like. Folks can't proclaim the glories of polygamy if they look at the experience of Leah. The sadness starts oozing out of the text in verse 30, 'And he loved Rachel rather than Leah.'

How often sheer sadness and mere misery blight human lives! One thinks of Winston Churchill as a child, writing his pathetic letters to his mother, begging her to come and visit him at his school – weeks and years of such letters, but she never found time. Or there was Anthony Ashley Cooper (Lord Shaftesbury), whose parents not only ignored but apparently detested their children, making Ashley wish he could blot out their memory.[5] Then how frequently we hear of the sad lot of Christ's servants in our own time. Here is a young woman in central Asia. She decided to follow Jesus and began attending church. When her Muslim husband heard, he beat her severely and then threw her out of the house along with their two small children. She went to her parents, but her father threw her out and sent her back to her husband. The husband kept the children but threw her out again.[6] Such joylessness may not be an occasional matter but, like Leah's, may cloud years of one's life.

Psalm 88 is unique in that, unlike most other 'lament' psalms, it does not conclude on a note of renewed hope. It's still dark at the end of the psalm. Derek Kidner draws an inference from this; he says the psalm witnesses to 'the possibility of unrelieved suffering as a believer's earthly lot.'[7] We cringe at

---

5. Cf. on these, Robert K. Massie, *Dreadnought* (New York: Random House, 1991), pp. 750-53; and Gaius Davies, *Genius, Grief and Grace* (Rossshire: Christian Focus, 2001), pp. 124-27.

6. From a Barnabas Aid prayer guide.

7. In *Psalms 73-150* (London: Inter-Varsity, 1975), p. 319. However, we must remember that Psalm 88 records a slice of the believer's experience up to the moment; we don't know but that relief may have come later.

that and yet it seems that a certain wretchedness must have dogged Leah through much of her life. It is pitiful indeed when 'no one cares for my soul' (Ps. 142:4) sums up one's life. And, if we are on the 'outside' of such experience, there's often nothing we can do to 'fix' the problem for someone, though heart-broken intercessory prayers are always in order.

6

A BIBLICAL SOAP OPERA
(Genesis 29:31–30:24)

The premier truth of this section is that *the covenant God remains faithful in and in spite of the slop and messes of the covenant people.* And the particular mess in this text really took off that night when Laban slipped Leah into the honeymoon bed and Jacob woke up to realize, 'Oh, no! It was Leah!' (29:25).[1] I hope you do not laugh at that – at least if Leah were here, it would cut her to the heart. Yes, let's begin with Leah and notice …

The People God Helps: The Justice of God (29:31-35)

A check of the pertinent articles in the *New Bible Dictionary* (3rd ed., 1996) will reveal that 'Leah' receives seventeen lines, while 'Rachel' gets parts of three columns. Leah would say, 'Well, that's how it's always been.' Verse 31 tells us that 'Yahweh saw that Leah was hated.' How was she hated? Remember verse 30: Jacob 'loved Rachel rather than Leah.' But when Yahweh

---

1. We can't know for sure, I suppose, but I doubt that Leah was willingly complicit in Laban's deception; likely she was more of a trapped pawn. She probably had little choice but to do 'what Dad said.' One gets the impression that one did not cross Laban's wishes.

sees He also acts: he 'opened Her womb' (v. 31) and four sons were born. The Bible knows the human mechanics of conception and birth, but it also knows that it is ultimately Yahweh's doing that gives such conception and birth.

Leah usually gives 'Yahweh interpretations' to the births. 'Yahweh has looked upon my affliction,' she says (v. 32). The name Reuben is a play on the verb for 'to look,' or 'to see.' 'Yahweh has heard I am hated' (v. 33), she said, and named the second son Simeon, a play on the verb 'to hear.' She thought Jacob might be drawn to her after the third birth, or hoped he would, 'Now this time my husband will be joined to me' (v. 34). The name Levi is a play on the verb 'to be joined.' But these are most likely simply sad and pitiful notes, perhaps more wistful than really hopeful: 'Now my husband will love me' (v. 32), and 'Now this time my husband will be joined to me' (v. 34). These are the heartaches of a woman who is fertile but otherwise unwanted.

The writer, however, has given us a peek at what God is doing. 'When Yahweh saw that Leah was hated he opened her womb' (v. 31). Here is the God who is at work and who shows that He is *for* the despised, the neglected, the wronged, the used. So Leah gives birth and, among others, bears the forerunners of the priestly and kingly tribes (Levi, 34; Judah, 35). Is this not a bit of the justice of God?

Jesus shows the same pattern. Here is this woman being berated for her lavish 'waste' of all her ointment on Jesus (Mark 14:1-9). And Jesus immediately takes up her case: 'Leave her alone! Why are you making trouble for her?' (v. 6). God is like this all through history to the end. The martyrs of the fifth seal in Revelation 6:9-10 assume that the God of His despised and trashed people will put things right for them, and Revelation 16:5-6 shows that He does. But right here God takes up the case for Leah, and there's something attractive about a God who is just.

Hank Aaron is well-known in American baseball lore. He had a star-studded career with the Milwaukee (later, Atlanta) Braves. However, Aaron's early days in baseball, in the early 1950s, were spent in the minor leagues and many of these teams were located in the south. Black players, like Aaron, had to deal with the hard face of segregation. Which meant that if the team stopped at a restaurant to eat, the three black players had to stay on the bus; some of the white players would order hamburgers for them and bring them out to the bus. They couldn't eat in a 'white' restaurant. They couldn't stay with the rest of the team in a 'normal' hotel – they were either farmed out to black families in the community or put up at another, run-down hotel in a run-down area. Ben Geraghty was the team manager, a white fellow, who knew baseball inside out but was hardly the most debonair specimen of humanity. But Aaron and the other black players had an immense affection for Geraghty. Once when the team was in Columbus, Georgia, they were invited out to Fort Benning. Time came to eat, and Aaron and the other two blacks are suddenly shuttled off to the kitchen. But as soon as they sit down to eat by themselves, here comes Ben Geraghty to sit and eat with them. Whenever the team stayed overnight somewhere, Geraghty would always go over to the seedy hotel where his black players had to stay and visit with them there.[2] Geraghty couldn't overturn the shackles of segregation, but he could show that he stood with his black players, liked them, and had no qualms about sharing their circumstances. They knew he was *for* them. And there's something wonderful about that.

Still, it may seem like quite a stretch to move from God's intervention in Leah's case to the assurance that He will also put things right for His downtrodden people at large and at

2. Henry Aaron (with Lonnie Wheeler), *I Had a Hammer* (New York: HarperCollins, 1991), pp. 64-65.

last. But if God is 'faithful in little' (cf. Luke 16:10), will He not also be faithful in much? Is this not the reason He is the hope of such believers today in communist China, North Korea, Nigeria, and Iran, for example? Can any other kind of God be our hope? 'And will not God surely bring about justice for his elect who cry out to him day and night, though he delays long over them?' (Luke 18:7). Next, note …

The Pleas God Hears: The Kindness of God (30:1-24)

Prayer seems as far from this narrative as Glasgow from Los Angeles, and, at any rate, we need to wade through the trash talk and tension of this domestic brouhaha first. So we look at the story and face Rachel's frustration and her envy of Leah. 'Give me children,' she moans to Jacob, 'or I'm going to die' (v. 1). Her demand burns Jacob up, and he retorts with 'Am I in the place of God who has held back the fruit of the womb from you?' (v. 2). Jacob scores high on theology but low on sensitivity. This is the initial blow-up. It may be (though who can tell?) that Jacob pointed out that the trouble was not with him; he was, after all, having children by Leah. Did he say, '*I'm* not the problem, Rachel'? Rachel then resorts to the Bilhah technique (vv. 3-8); she will give her maid to Jacob as a secondary wife, but the children will be technically allotted to Rachel. It worked. Along come Dan and Naphtali.

Leah forms a ditto-plan (vv. 9-13). She had 'ceased bearing' after her four sons (29:35).[3] She gives Zilpah, her maid, to Jacob's bed and Leah's tally then includes Gad and Asher (= Lucky and Happy).

Verses 14-16 tell about the 'mandrake madness.' Reuben, Leah's oldest, finds some mandrakes and brings them to his

---

3. This may have been naturally the case, or, as some expositors think, Jacob may have ceased sexual relations with her.

mother.[4] These plants produce a bluish flower in winter and yellow plum-size fruit in summer, carry a distinct fragrance, and were thought to increase sexual desire and chances of fertility. The text doesn't endorse this view; it was popular lore. So Rachel asks for some of Leah's 'fertility drugs' (v. 14). This aggravates Leah – Rachel already has Jacob in her bed all the time and now she wants some of Leah's fertility aids (v. 15a). Rachel proposes a deal. Things get quite earthy here. If Leah gives Rachel some mandrakes, she'll allow Leah to have Jacob in bed that night (v. 15b). Leah gets Jacob as 'stud for the night' (v. 16) – and Leah gets pregnant (v. 17). In fact, she gives birth to Issachar, Zebulon, and Dinah (vv. 17-21). Yet there is still the sad refrain of failing to win Jacob's attention or affection (v. 20). Then, at last, God 'remembered' Rachel and she gave birth to Joseph (vv. 22-24).

That's a synopsis of the story, but now we note the interpretations. My father used to repeat a quote: 'Figures won't lie, but liars will figure.' By the same token, theologians won't manipulate, but manipulators will theologize. And Leah and Rachel each have their own spin for their circumstances. After Dan's birth from Bilhah, Rachel declares, 'God has given judgment for me, and what's more, he has heard my voice and given me a son' (30:6). Did God vindicate Rachel in that birth? Is that what this birth shows? It's what Rachel claims, at any rate. At Issachar's birth, Leah claims that 'God has given (me) my wages because I gave my maid to my husband' (30:18). Hmm …. Are you sure you have that right, Leah? These are the 'theological' assertions of the characters in this family feud, but assertions by the characters are not the same as affirmations by the text.

---

4. Some dispute whether the mandrakes were mandrakes, since they were not common in Mesopotamia. But see G. J. Wenham, *Genesis 16-50*, WBC (Dallas: Word, 1994), pp. 246-47.

However, the text does tell us what God was doing, and, though Leah and Rachel may have erred in some of their theologizing, the writer shows that they have been right in divining that God has been there. Note the testimony of verse 17 – 'God listened to Leah and she became pregnant ….' That's not Leah's claim but the text's assertion. And it comes right after the crass deal in which Leah buys Jacob's services for the night. Yet mixed up in all of that there must have been Leah's pleas to God for more children. Then there's the clear statement of verse 22, 'Then God remembered Rachel, and God listened to her and opened her womb.' Hence Joseph. Apparently, Rachel had been long pleading for children. Put these statements together in the context. In face of pawning off maids and bargaining for fertility aids, God listened. No explicit prayers are expressed; yet God listened. Likely their desires were expressed in prayers that may have been riddled with their plots and schemes and jealousies. But God heard. Their pleas did not arise from fine motives; they came from aching hearts – and God heard.

You may be tempted to arrogance here, knowing that you are more sophisticated in the arena of prayer. You may think Rachel and Leah need tutoring on the finer points of prayer, blind to the fact that you may suffer from the same or similar malady. You could be like congressman Nelson Dingley from Maine who was holding forth in the House of Representatives, speaking on behalf of a tariff bill and denouncing Americans who evaded the 'rigors of the custom laws' by making their purchases abroad. At which point Jerry Simpson of Kansas reached under Dingley's desk, pulled out Dingley's hat and held it up so everyone could see the label: 'Made in London.'[5]

We admit it then: we ourselves let loose with some pretty screwed-up prayers. Leah and Rachel are not the only ones who

---

5. Paul Boller, *Congressional Anecdotes* (New York: Oxford, 1991), p. 202.

have trouble getting prayer straight. Isn't that the testimony of Romans 8:26? That comes before verse 28 where Paul says, 'And we know …'. But in verse 26 there is something 'we do not know' – we do not know what to pray for as we ought.[6] Can't look down on Leah and Rachel when we are such bumblers ourselves. And … if we only received when we got our prayers and motives all right, would we ever receive from the hand of God? Praise God that God hears, that He hears and interprets and answers cries from aching hearts that have trouble getting their motives straight. Here is the sheer kindness of God. Finally, looking at this account in its larger context, we note …

The Promise God Fulfills: The Faithfulness of God

You must understand that there is far more in this account than family turmoil and a saga of domestic sex and reproduction. It's something like the time when Marlon Brando was making his first film (*The Men* [1950]), a movie about World War II veterans who'd lost their legs in combat. So that he could learn much more about them he lived in a wheelchair for a while with some army-hospital paraplegics. One day he went to a pub with some of them for drinks, and a Salvation Army lady came in to collect some waste paper. When she saw these legless veterans in wheelchairs, she was shocked and raised her hands and cried, 'O Lord, grant that these men may be able to walk again!' At which point Brando got up and walked, and the woman nearly passed out.[7] There was far more there that she imagined.

What is the 'far more' in this narrative? It goes back to the promise to Abraham to make him a 'great nation' so that God could give the land to his 'seed' (12:2, 7). His 'seed' was Isaac.

---

6. The text speaks not of the 'how' of prayer but of the 'what'.

7. Paul F. Boller, Jr. and Ronald L. Davis, *Hollywood Anecdotes* (New York: William Morrow, 1987), p. 141.

Isaac had the same promise (26:4) and his seed was Jacob. Jacob receives the same promise (28:14) – and this chapter shows that his seed consists of *eleven* sons. That's light years away from being like the dust of the earth or the stars of the sky, but it's a lot closer than single-digit Abraham and Isaac ever got. It's the 'people' aspect of the promise and in the middle of all this furor Yahweh is beginning to fulfill it in a marked way.

You've read it all: husband and wife yelling at each other, bedroom rivalry, the covenant family in all its dysfunctional glory. Yet in spite of all the crabbing, strife, conflict, anguish, tensions, bickering, and miseries – through it all, *in* it all, Yahweh is faithful to His promise; here are eleven sons. Does this mean that God approves of having four wives? No. The text *reports* that Jacob did, but the text is not thereby *recommending* that to God's people. In fact, the obvious misery of this family suggests the writer is dead set against multiple wives. Does God's faithfulness justify the envy that keeps pushing for the most-fertile-female award? No, the fact of Yahweh's fidelity to His Word does not sanitize all the circumstances or attitudes of His people. But you've got to see it. In all the slop the 'seed' is multiplying. Not the dust of the earth yet but a lot closer than Abraham and Isaac ever got. Who would have thought, who could have guessed, that a bizarre soap opera would proclaim the faithfulness of God?

But the Bible seems to thrive on such combinations. It's something like the time Winston Churchill took a cab to a meeting. The cab driver drew up at the address, and Churchill didn't get out. The Cockney cabbie hollered, 'You 'ave arrived, governor. You're 'ere.' Churchill put him off with: 'I know. I know. I'm just preparing my impromptu remarks.'[8]

---

8. James C. Humes, *The Sir Winston Method* (New York: William Morrow, 1991), p. 114.

'Impromptu' remarks that are 'prepared'? It seems oxymoronic. But no more than chaos and providence, confusion and faithfulness, or jealousy and sovereignty.

So we come back to the beginning: *The triumphant chemistry of divine providence takes the sludge and mess of our affairs and produces the fruit of His faithfulness.* I can't go further with this principle right now. I can only ask if you've found this faithful God working like this in your own life. You remember that time – perhaps years ago – that time filled with the din of your anger, your envy, your lusts, your stupidity, your ambition and blindness and perhaps rage, but you have since discovered, now you have seen it, that God was there in all that gunk in His quiet faithfulness. How can you help but adore such a God?

7

ALMOST EXODUS TIME
(Genesis 30:25–31:21)

In a 'Peanuts' cartoon Lucy is on her hands and knees and Linus is standing beside her. Lucy tells Linus to 'look at this tiny little bug' she is scrutinizing. She begins to editorialize: 'It's appalling how little he knows ... he's not like us ... he doesn't know anything about voting, or disease, or earthquakes, or love or Monday mornings.' And Linus retorts, 'Who's better off?' Coming to the present passage, however, an interpreter feels he's in something of a 'bug' dilemma. It's not that he can't understand what the text is reporting (at least on the whole – there are 'iffy' issues), but it's a bit baffling to discern what Yahweh is doing in these episodes. If the primary focus of the text should be on revealing Yahweh, either in His character or activity, how do we see that here? At first sight this passage may seem concerned with little more than labor agreements, successful livestock breeding, deteriorating family relations, and a need to 'move house.' And like Lucy's bug, we may be unable to discern more. Except ... there are some hints one can detect and I want you to consider them.

First, ponder both Laban and Jacob's words when they speak of **Yahweh's obvious blessing** (30:25-30). Laban is like some people we know – he's so wrapped up in his own concerns that he doesn't 'hear' what someone tells him. Laban thinks every man has his price. His response to Jacob's request to leave Paddan-aram is 'Let's make a deal' (v. 28). But in verse 27 Laban indicates why he is loath for Jacob to leave: 'I have become rich and Yahweh has blessed me because of you.'[1] For once Jacob can agree with Laban: 'The little you had before I came has exploded, so Yahweh has blessed you wherever I turned' (v. 30). Sly guy and cool customer as he is, Laban can tell the difference between 'before' and 'after,' has to admit that Yahweh's blessing seems to stick to Jacob's presence, and he'd be a fool to let him leave his employ.

In a sense this is how it was supposed to be. Yahweh had originally told Abram, 'In you all the families of the ground will be blessed' (12:3). This was the 'program' aspect of Yahweh's fourfold promise. But such blessing was not only something for the distant future but Abram himself, for example, was to 'be a blessing' (12:2). Already in Genesis Abraham both was – and wasn't. He was not a blessing to Pharaoh (12:17-20) nor to Abimelech (at least initially, ch. 20), but he was in rescuing Lot & Co. (14:14-16) and in interceding for residents of Sodom and Gomorrah (chs. 18-19). Jacob then is a means of blessing to Laban (our current text); and Joseph became a channel of blessing to Pharaoh in revealing what future days would bring (chs. 40–41) and to Jacob's family in preserving their lives (ch. 45) – indeed, a blessing to all Egypt (47:13-26).

The paradigm still operates. The world does sometimes realize that it receives blessing because of and through covenant people. And it doesn't always occur in any highly visible or sensational way. I recall a summer when I had worked in a Pennsylvania state park, checking in campers and

---

1. 'I have become rich' adopts a rendering based on an Akkadian cognate; the traditional translation has been, 'I have learned by divination.' Cf. G. J. Wenham, *Genesis 16-50*, WBC (Dallas: Word, 1994), pp. 250-51, 255.

collecting fees from them. Near the end of August it was time to head back to college. The park superintendent indicated his appreciation for my work and told me that when I was working he 'never had to worry about the cash drawer.' It was just simple honesty. But he knew whose name I professed and through me he received benefit, however miniscule it might seem. Call it 'blessing' with a small 'b.' Much more could be said but the principle is clear: Yahweh's blessing sticks to Yahweh's people and is meant to be unloaded on those in Yahweh's world.

I would suggest a second emphasis in this text which we might call **Yahweh's precarious work** (30:31-43 mainly, with a bit of help from ch. 31). We'll come back to this emphasis later, but first let's summarize what's happening in the story.

Jacob proposes that he should take the odd or rare type animals from Laban's flock, that is, 'every dark-colored sheep and every spotted and speckled goat' (30:32, NJPS). Sheep and lambs were predominantly white, goats normally dark, so Jacob proposes that he be given only the rare types. Sounds massively reasonable and Laban agrees (v. 34). But Laban is a hustler. He no sooner shakes hands on the deal than he culls these rare specimens from the flock and puts his sons in charge of them at a three-days' journey away (vv. 35-36). It seems that Laban has just taken away the 'starter pool' that Jacob could use for the start of his own holdings. But Jacob has his own breeding technique, strange as it strikes us, to produce 'odd' types (vv. 37-40). Was this a folk-belief that a visual sight of peeled branches in watering troughs would produce streaked, speckled, and spotted young? Apparently; though the text does not endorse it but simply notes Jacob practiced it. But whatever we make of the belief or method doesn't much matter; verse 39 clearly states what happened – the pro-Jacob result.[2] Then

---

2. Some expositors hold that Jacob may well have been more astute than simply following popular belief; cf., e.g., V. P. Hamilton, *The Book of Genesis: Chapters 18-50,* NICOT (Grand Rapids: Eerdmans, 1995), p. 284,

Jacob included some selective breeding (vv. 41-42) which gave him sturdier stock and Laban more anemic specimens.

Jacob's 'nevertheless' success seems to have led to Laban's repeatedly flipflopping on the terms of the agreement (31:7-8), to no avail. The 'ten times' Jacob claims Laban changed his wages is probably not meant as a precise number but somewhat akin to Calvin's lament about Geneva (before he was expelled), that 'not a day has passed in which I did not ten times wish for death'! The tremendous success Jacob enjoyed (30:43) points to God's giving him justice in the face of all Laban's devious moves. At least that was Jacob's interpretation (31:9) and we've no reason to doubt it.

And yet. Though there was nothing dishonest in Jacob's breeding program, there's a clear hint that Jacob is still Jacob. His selective breeding in 30:41-42 in which he ensured that his flocks were the sturdier and Laban's the weaker, though not technically 'wrong,' still shows that Jacob is always concerned to look out for 'number one.' Laban may be the villain, but Jacob is hardly Mr. Clean. And here is where God's 'precarious work' comes in. It seems He chooses to give Jacob success and to frustrate Laban's designs even though Jacob is no paragon of virtue himself. Yahweh is a 'risk-taking' God who works justice in Jacob's behalf even though Jacob is no sanitized, pasteurized, sanctified servant who is completely consecrated and has totally 'surrendered all.' Does he have to be? If receiving Yahweh's favor were dependent on our being in a consistently proper condition, would Yahweh not forever be stifling His goodness? Does He force Himself to wait until we are rightly up to standard?

During the War Between the States in my country George B. McClellan was over the northern 'Army of the Potomac.'

---

and Andrew E. Steinmann, *Genesis*, TOTC (London: Inter-Varsity, 2019), pp. 289-90. Verse 40 is difficult, but the whole scenario is clear enough.

Troops admired McClellan; he was a superb administrator and unmatched at whipping an army into shape. He was also immeasurably arrogant and full of disdain for President Lincoln and associates. He had always been successful in life, just as he was with preparing his army. But when the time came to act, to fight, he was woefully reluctant and always keen to project blame on to others. He was, as historian James McPherson claims, 'afraid to risk failure.' 'McClellan excelled at preparation, but it was never quite complete. The army was perpetually *almost* ready to move – but the enemy was always larger and better prepared.'[3] For McClellan, everything had to be just right, and all contingencies nailed down before he would act. And so he didn't – and squandered his opportunities.

Thankfully, Yahweh is not like that. He will risk bringing His help and blessing even to servants who don't have their spiritual virtues all zipped up. Think, for example, of those Hebrew Christians who had not made the progress in maturity that they should have (Heb. 5:11-12; 6:1-3), who seemed to be fearful about coming out from behind the protective shadow of Judaism and standing full-bore for Jesus. And yet their pastor told them, 'For God is not unjust; He will not forget your work and the love you showed for His name when you served the saints—and you continue to serve them' (Heb. 6:10, HCSB). The Lord's people are – perhaps we could say – as speckled and spotted as Jacob's goats but that does not clog up the flow of His grace and help to us in the muck and mire of our troubles. He is willing to take the risk.

Lastly, let us note **Yahweh's clear call** (31:3, 13). Relations with Laban and his sons are breaking down – they eye Jacob with envy and hostility. So, at this point, Yahweh intervenes and tells Jacob, 'Go back to the land of your fathers and to

---

3. James M. McPherson, *Battle Cry of Freedom* (New York: Oxford, 1988), p. 365.

your relations, and I will be with you' (31:3). It seems that this call came via a dream-revelation (31:10-11). In verse 13 Jacob repeats the call he received to Rachel and Leah.

Matters proceed step-by-step. First comes *persuasion* (31:4-13). Jacob pow-wows with Rachel and Leah out in the field with the flock, away from prying ears. He rehearses the wrongs their father has inflicted on him and discloses how God has called him to head back to Canaan. Then follows *consent* (31:14-16). There seems to be plenty of love lost between these sisters and their father.[4] They see no future in staying under Laban's aegis. Then follows the *action* (31:17-21). Preparing to leave Paddan-aram would be quite a project, but it was done – conveniently, when Laban was off somewhere at his sheep-shearing duties. Another interesting combination: Yahweh's clear call and Jacob's devious departure.

That is the story: Yahweh issues a clear call to Jacob to engage in an 'exodus' and to return to the land of Canaan (cf. 28:15). I can't help but think of what use this story may have been years later to a later generation of Jacob's family. In this story Jacob is in a kind of bondage to Laban, has before him the possibility of escape with, of course, the risks and danger involved – yet clearly called by God to go. Think how this story may have 'spoken' to the Exodus 1–2 generation. Or imagine how Moses may have used this story as 'preaching

---

4. It's not completely clear what their complaint consists of in verses 14-15. IVPBBC (ed. Walton, Matthews, and Chavalas) highlights one option: 'It has been suggested that they are referring to assets that were generally held in escrow for the care of the woman should her husband die or divorce her. Such assets would have been part of the bride price, which, in this case, Jacob had paid in labor rather than tangible assets. If Laban never put aside the value of Jacob's fourteen years of labor, there would be nothing in reserve to provide for the women. As a result they would not enjoy any additional protection in economic terms by staying in the vicinity of their family. They identify this as treating them as foreigners, because Laban had gained from Jacob's labor but had not passed the gain on to them—it is therefore just as if he had sold them' (p. 63).

material' to stir them up to leave Egypt. He could say their situation had been faced before – their father Jacob had to escape from Laban's jurisdiction; it was fraught with all sorts of unknowns and risks, and yet under a clear call from God, just as the Israelites were (cf. Exod. 3:7-8). It was now time for another 'exodus,' Moses could now say. Would it not be a way of offering encouragement to perhaps hesitant slaves in Egypt?

We can't be sure Moses did use such earlier accounts as his preaching material. But it is at least plausible. Isn't this partly why Paul can speak of 'the encouragement of the Scriptures' (Rom. 15:4)? Not only didactic but even narrative sections of the Bible depict situations in which God's people find themselves, situations roughly similar to our own, and seeing God's call and provision in the Bible-situation is a tremendous encouragement to us in ours. Is this not at least one way in which we should read Scripture? When we read Ruth 1 and see how life caves in, how one can be so seemingly alone, is it not humongously [if the adjective is allowed, why not an adverb?] heartening to see how Yahweh's providence goes quietly to work? When we may be nearly paralyzed with fear, aren't we delighted to see how whether with Gideon (Judg. 7:9-15) or with Samuel (1 Sam. 16:2-3) Yahweh knows and stoops to meet the fears of His servants – without mocking them for their fears? When we're wondering why God takes so long to meet our dilemmas, don't we find Judges 13 helpful, when Yahweh seems to be in no hurry but *grows* a deliverer from scratch, even from a hitherto barren woman? When God's apparently 'irrational' ways throw us for a loop, doesn't Exodus 14:1-4 (making Israel sitting ducks for Pharaoh) or Joshua 5:2-3 (circumcising an army in enemy territory) at least assure us that others have faced this same perplexity? Yahweh seems to bend over backwards in order to encourage us by those who've gone before us.

8

ESCAPE FROM CHICANERY
(Genesis 31:22-55)

I have, nestled in the historical section of my library, a volume entitled *True Stories of Great Escapes*. It's a 'Reader's Digest' collection of over forty episodes of such escapes. And of course one finds such stories in the Bible. I once preached a short sermon series on 'Great Escapes of the Bible' and Jacob's escape from Laban in this text was the first in the series. What a mixed bag this story is! Here are trickery and justice, anger and suspicion, thievery and protection, scheming and escape, fury and peace. Yet in all this Yahweh is bringing His covenant servant back to covenant space, covenant man back to covenant land. Verses 17-21 report the escape itself. 'Mum' is the word – Jacob sees no need to tell Laban about the matter; indeed, Jacob seems up to his old tricks in that he waits to take off till Laban is preoccupied with sheep-shearing.[1] My concern here is to isolate the *testimony* this passage intends to give, and I think that testimony revolves around two major themes.

---

1. Sheep-shearing could be both an arduous and time-consuming task. For some examples from Mari texts, see V. P. Hamilton, *The Book of Genesis: Chapters 18-50*, NICOT (Grand Rapids: Eerdmans, 1995), p. 299.

The first theme we can call **hard protection** (vv. 22-29, 43-55). Laban receives word of Jacob's flight 'on the third day' (v. 22), likely the third day after Jacob had vamoosed. It then took Laban & Co seven days (v. 23) to catch up with Jacob's outfit in the hill country of Gilead east of the Jordan River. We must not assume too much here. There may well have been a gap between the day Laban heard and when he began his pursuit. Not likely that he would break off his sheep-shearing. He would probably complete that before his pursuit. So the seven days of Laban's pursuit do not necessarily immediately follow the three days of Jacob's head start.[2]

One can be excused for being cynical about Laban. He is all fluster and bluster. He claims Jacob has 'carried off' his daughters as if they were prisoners of war (v. 26). He rails at Jacob because the latter's devious departure has deprived him of throwing a proper send-off celebration (v. 27), as if the tight-wad were longing to underwrite such an occasion. Why should such a father and grandfather be robbed of saying a proper and fond farewell (v. 28)? If Laban wondered why Jacob had left (cf. v. 30), Jacob was perfectly candid: 'Because I was afraid' – afraid that Laban would 'tear away' his daughters from Jacob (v. 31). Translated, Jacob is saying, 'Because I have had no reason to trust you whatsoever; I wouldn't put anything past you.'

But all Laban's fury and ferocity is dead on arrival. We hear the reason for this three times, first from the writer (v. 24), then from Laban himself (v. 29), and finally confirmed by Jacob (v. 42b – 'my affliction and the toil of my hands God

---

2. Some think that 'seven' may not be an exact number but a figure that signifies a somewhat extensive period of time. In any case, assuming a strictly consecutive period of 10 days (3 + 7) is a problem. As John Currid points out, from Haran to the Gilead region is roughly 350 miles (for a crow) and it is unrealistic to imagine that Jacob's group could average 35 miles/day with flocks and goods (*A Study Commentary on Genesis*, 2 vols. [Darlington: Evangelical Press, 2003], 2:112-13).

saw and rebuked you last night'). The statement in verse 24 (and 29) is a bit awkward to translate: 'Watch yourself, that you not speak anything to Jacob from good to evil.' The sense seems to refer to the whole spectrum of speech, especially threatening talk. TEV probably catches the sense – 'Be careful not to threaten Jacob in any way.' God's threat stifles Laban's threats, as if he says, 'Laban, you mess with Jacob and you're street pizza.' So Laban yammers a bit more (v. 43), but all he can do is call for a treaty (v. 44), which primarily was a non-aggression pact (vv. 51-52).[3]

When Jacob agrees to this covenant/treaty, he swears by 'the *pachad* of Isaac' (v. 53b). The word is a very strong 'fear' word, often connoting dread or terror.[4] Some may be hesitant to take this as referring to God, but in this context it makes excellent sense. Jacob's God is 'the Dreadful One of Isaac,' the one who inspires and causes dread, terror, or fear. That is precisely what God does in verses 24 and 29. He is the God who intimidates Laban, who threatens him should he try to harm Jacob in any way. He so much as says: If you threaten Jacob, Laban, it'll be the last thing you do; you harm Jacob and you're toast. Laban has met God the Intimidator.

Sometimes God still uses His Laban-technique and gives His sheer, naked, out-of-the-blue protection to His helpless servants. Maria Linke lived in Berlin and was married there just prior to World War II. After the war she was taken captive

---

3. The words of verse 49 seem to be Laban's, fleshing out one of the names for the place, Mizpah (= watch tower) with 'Yahweh watch between you and me, while we are absent [hidden] one from the other.' When I was a young teenager, our church youth meetings were closed by repeating what was called the 'Mizpah benediction' (= v. 49). At the time I did not realize it was anything but a benediction! In its context it almost means, 'May the Lord keep His eye on us – especially on you, you low-life scoundrel.' But not knowing or bothering about the context we would go on piously intoning those words weekly at the close of a meeting.

4. Cf. TWOT, 2:720-21.

by the Russians and incarcerated in one of their prison camps from 1945-54. There she was interrogated and beaten, kicked and stomped on. Her interrogators wanted her to become a propagandist to build the East German regime and she refused to comply. On one occasion she told the Lieutenant (Khorobrov) that she as a believer in God could not, in principle, work for or advocate an atheistic regime. So Khorobrov went to his holster and pulled out his pistol. She looked into its dark barrel as he asked, 'Do you still believe in God?' Maria told him his bullets had nothing to do with the matter, that he couldn't kill her unless 'God allows it,' that she was prepared to die and he would have to answer for the matter. He pulled the trigger – and nothing happened. 'No explosion, no blinding flash of light, no angels' song, no sudden entrance into God's presence.' There was only an angry, bald-headed, foolish-looking little man fuming over a useless gun. He made all the adjustments, pulled the trigger again. Nothing. He threw the pistol across the floor and ordered her to get out.[5] There are all kinds of such amazing and validated accounts. Oh, we know. Usually the gun goes off; usually the torture ruins and destroys. But sometimes God simply imposes His hard protection, His 'Laban move,' on behalf of His people.

I suppose we can see why He did that in Genesis 31. Here is Jacob and his relatively small clan – not necessarily sanitized or highly sanctified but all the 'church' there is at this point in the world. Could Laban have smashed them? Apparently so. But if Jacob and company go belly up, God's people cease to exist in this world. So when threatened and powerless with no other help, God intervenes to protect. Even though God doesn't usually grant such 'hard protection' to His people, this text is nevertheless the comfort of His suffering church, because it tells them that Yahweh will never allow them to

---

5. Ruth Hunt, *East Wind* (Grand Rapids: Zondervan, 1976), pp. 163-64.

be extinguished. It was the Waldenses, that battered and slaughtered people, who nevertheless in their 1655 confession of faith said that [we believe] 'that this Church can not fail, nor be annihilated, but must endure forever.'[6]

The second theme in our passage is **vicious sarcasm** (vv. 30-42). Suddenly, in the middle of his tirade (vv. 26-30a), Laban switches subjects ('Why did you steal my gods?' v. 30b). He does so without even a conjunction – there is no 'But' before 'why' in the Hebrew (as in, e.g., ESV). He knows he must not touch Jacob, but he can certainly demand his rights in a matter of theft.

Let's make a few observations. First, what a ridiculous question Laban asks! What sort of deities are they if they can be effortlessly pilfered? What helpless things (cf. Judg. 18:24). Second, ignorance brings such tension into the situation. Jacob boldly declares that if Laban finds his gods with anyone of his entourage, that person 'will not live' (v. 32). Then we are told that Jacob didn't know Rachel had 'lifted' them (v. 32b). What Jacob did not know could hurt him. What irony seems to leak out of the text here!

Third, readers want to know why Rachel swiped these idols. When verse 19 tells of Rachel's theft it calls them *teraphim,* apparently 'household idols.' In this case they were small images since Rachel could stash them in the camel's saddle (v. 34). One meets various answers regarding Rachel's motive. Some think possession of such deities had something to do with family inheritance or leadership, others think they may have been looked on as protection deities. I doubt Rachel looked on them as protective – that she sits on them (v. 34) seems to convey a lack of respect. I think Rachel stole them simply because Laban ticked Rachel off; she knew he prized

---

6. Article 26. See Philip Schaff, *The Creeds of Christendom*, 3 vols. (Grand Rapids: Baker, 1990 reprint), 3:765.

these *teraphim* and she wanted to gall him and drive him up a wall.[7] Not everything needs to be explained via Near Eastern parallels; it may be a matter of simple (and accumulating) animosity.

Fourth, these idols are both *warm* and, if we believe Rachel, *unclean* (vv. 34-35). Warm, because Rachel is sitting on them, unclean, because, as she 'apologizes' to Laban, 'Sorry, Dad, but I'm having my period.' A later Israelite at least hearing this story would view it through the requirements of Leviticus 15:19-30 (note especially v. 20). Everything a menstruating woman sits or lies on becomes technically 'unclean.' As Waltke says, these 'gods' were the equivalent of a sanitary napkin.[8] A devout worshiper of Yahweh would, I think, find this a real 'howler.' Any Israelite with a tad of humor would split his sides laughing. Gods that are both warm and impure!

Then, fifth, Laban's failure (v. 35b) sets Jacob off in his own blistering tirade of seven verses (vv. 36-42). He has probably 'practiced' this speech for some time, simply biding his time until he can 'vent' on Laban. It all erupts when it seems, at least to Jacob, that even Laban's charge about stolen gods is just more malarkey (v. 35b).[9] Jacob felt he needed to tell Laban that he was one huge hunk of low-down Mesopotamian scum.

Those are the observations. What seems to be the driving point of the episode? I should think it is the mockery of idols, of false gods. The text implies that idolatry is ludicrous, but when the Bible is 'humorous' it is also serious. And we, probably like

---

7. Since Rachel and Leah agree with Jacob's negative assessment of Laban (31:14-16), it's not likely Rachel cherishes any endearing affection for her father. It might be that she also disdained him for dumping Leah on Jacob (29:23-25) with all the attendant misery that brought – though we can't be sure because the text is silent on this score.

8. B. K. Waltke, *Genesis: A Commentary* (Grand Rapids: Zondervan, 2001), p. 430.

9. Don't miss Jacob's description of a shepherd's life in verses 38-41a; it was hardly a placid, back-to-nature lark.

Laban, may not see our idolatry at all. We are Anglicans or Baptists or Presbyterians or Pentecostals and our idolatry is much more sophisticated. Rachel can't sit on our idols.

We can't parade all our idols. But one is likely security. We may especially fixate on this when we don't seem to have much of it. This concern can dominate the decisions we make and the directions we take. I remember a friend telling me about one of his church members who had a higher echelon job in a company. But he resigned from it. One of his responsibilities was to secure prostitutes for visiting executives and he refused to do it. But to let go of that job? 'Security' must have tempted him to bow down.

Then some of us may be slaves of recognition. I usually don't sing part of 'Be Thou My Vision.' One stanza begins, 'Riches I heed not, nor man's empty praise.' Riches don't bother me much, but 'man's empty praise'? I'll take all I can get, thank you, empty or not. If only Rachel could sit on that!

Of course, some of our 'household gods' come in the humblest of guises. Ours is a psychological age and we hear much of self-esteem. It is, I suppose, a legitimate concern. You are not, after all, a hunk of junk. But is it not possible for your concern for self-esteem to control your whole life? If someone does not 'affirm' you and coddle you and treat you the way you want, you become disappointed and angry and maybe, just maybe, you realize that your passion for self-esteem has become your deity of choice and, obviously, a very fragile one at that. So…we may end up making our 'needs' our god. The prayer in William Cowper's hymn ('O For a Closer Walk with God') should be ours:

> The dearest idol I have known,
> Whate'er that idol be;
> Help me to tear it from thy throne,
> And worship only thee.

The trouble is that we cannot usually see these idols unless the Holy Spirit unleashes some of His scathing sarcasm and exposes the helpless things. It's a saving work when the Holy Spirit starts making fun of our idols.

The teaching of this passage can be summed up in two statements: (1) God will certainly preserve His people in this world – a word of comfort; and (2) 'Little children, keep yourselves from idols' (1 John 5:21) – a word of correction.

9

PREPARING FOR YOUR WORST NIGHTMARE
(Genesis 32:1-21)

Fear can paralyze. I know I've alluded to it before, but I found this out when a new Methodist minister moved to our western Pennsylvania town. His name was John Galbreath, and his wife was, obviously, Mrs. Galbreath. Normally, she wouldn't have been a problem but in our little community three of the churches met together on Sunday evenings for 'Union evening services,' meeting by turns a month in the Presbyterian, then the United Presbyterian (our franchise), and Methodist buildings. I was something like eight years old, was with my mother after an evening service, and she and Mrs. Galbreath were speaking with one another. Mrs. G spoke to me, and I did not return the greeting. I was shy, especially of older women. After perhaps several episodes of my non-response, she, one evening, told me that if I did not speak to her next time, she would kiss me. She said this in a jocular sort of way, but she had no idea the impact she was having. Sheer, unmitigated terror. Every Sunday evening, nothing but dread. The second after the benediction I bolted for the door to escape her clutches – and lips. Fear and dread hovered over every Sunday evening. I was having my worst nightmare.

In this text Jacob faces his worst nightmare – Esau. Rebekah had implied years ago that Esau would forget what Jacob had done to him (27:44-45). Fat chance! Laban had returned home (31:55b). That problem was over, Laban was out of the picture, but now Esau filled the whole canvas and Jacob seemed quite sure that he had not forgotten. Jacob is facing what he thinks is his worst nightmare. Jacob is returning at God's command (31:3), as Andrew Steinmann reminds us, but that did not dissolve his fear. Jesus' disciples got into the boat at Jesus' command (Mark 4:35) and it nearly scared them to death. One can obey God and get into huge trouble. Let's walk through Jacob's experience and consider several pieces of it.

First, notice in verses 1–2 **the place of timely encouragement.** As Jacob journeys on, 'the angels of God met him'; Jacob explains that 'This is God's camp!'; and names the location 'Mahanaim,' a dual form meaning 'two camps.' I assume he means the camp of the angels of God and the camp of Jacob. We recall that when Jacob was exiting the land, he dreamed and saw the angels of God in that dream (28:12), while here he is re-entering the land and the angels met him, apparently in some visible form.[1] He is not on his own. He has protection. This should be a genuine encouragement to him with Esau on the horizon.

Perhaps this doesn't seem like much encouragement to us, but then sometimes it doesn't take much to keep us going. The American illustrator and artist, Norman Rockwell, endured a disappointing childhood. He was not muscular or athletic nor were his marks in school much above passing. But his eighth-

---

1. Calvin makes a little hay out of the plural form 'angels': 'for although a single angel would suffice as a guardian for us, yet the Lord acts more liberally towards us. Therefore they who think that each of us is defended by one angel only, wickedly depreciate the kindness of God' (*Genesis*, 2 vols. in one [reprint ed., Edinburgh: Banner of Truth, 1975], 2:186).

grade teacher, Miss Julia Smith, recognized his artistic ability. She would have him come up to the blackboard and chalk out illustrations that supplemented her teaching of American history or science. She fussed over Rockwell's drawings, made him feel he had a real ability that somehow made up for his failure in baseball. Small wonder that he kept in touch with her for the rest of her life.[2] Her support may seem a relatively minor matter, but it made a major difference to Rockwell. In the same way, this 'angel collision' should have put fresh courage into Jacob as he faced the prospect of meeting Esau. Indeed, this seems to be a pattern in God's ways – providing fresh support in face of a coming need.

Think of Jesus at His baptism. John's baptism was a 'baptism of repentance' and in submitting to it Jesus was showing He was willing (already) to stand in the sinner's place. Think of the Father's voice at Jesus' baptism: 'You are my Son, the One I love – I am delighted with you!' (Mark 1:11). But then Mark's favorite adverb, 'Immediately,' introduces the strange sequence of the Spirit 'driving' Jesus into the wilderness to face Satan's temptations (vv. 12-13). Think how much His Father's words (v. 11) must've meant to Jesus in that distress and duress. How it must have heartened Him to ponder 'I am delighted with you!' and 'the One I love.' The Father's assurance bolstered Him to face the devil's onslaught. That is the sort of thing we see in this Jacob text: the competence of God to provide in light of the need He knows we will face. And we never know what form the 'angels' or the encouragement will take.

Secondly, consider **the place of candid prayer** in verses 9-13a. But before we look at Jacob's prayer, we must note his fresh emergency in verses 3-6. Jacob sent messengers to Esau; they were to tell Esau (1) who Jacob was, 'your servant' (v. 4a),

---

2. Deborah Solomon, *American Mirror: The Life and Art of Norman Rockwell* (New York: Farrar, Straus and Giroux, 2013), pp. 34-35.

(2) why he is now arriving – 'I have stayed with Laban and have been delayed until now' (v. 4b), (3) what he has (v. 5a, livestock and people), and (4) what he wants ('to find grace in your eyes,' v. 5b). Jacob's men come back with the news that Esau is on his way to meet Jacob – with 400 men! As someone has said, that spells 'raid'. So Jacob divides his people and stock into two groups, hoping perhaps to salvage one from Esau's scourge (vv. 7-8). Then we have four verses of Jacob's prayer, perhaps a good model for praying in our emergencies. How then should we pray?

First, *call on His name.* See how Jacob begins: 'O God of my father Abraham and God of my father Isaac' (v. 9a). This 'invocation' implies that Jacob's God has a 'history,' a past in which he proved faithful to Jacob's forbears before Jacob ever came along. So too, for us. You are not coming to an unskilled God, to some divine 'intern' seeking to gain experience by dealing with your case. Jacob is coming to an Abraham-and-Isaac-God who has taken those servants through all sorts of heavy weather and kept them on their feet.

Second, *plead His promises.* In verse 9b, Jacob recalls Yahweh's command-cum-promise: 'Return to your land and to your relatives, and I will deal well with you.' Then in verse 12 Jacob comes down all the more on Yahweh's promise. In face of the fear he acknowledges, he pleads, 'But *you* [emphatic] have said, "I will certainly do you good, and I shall make your seed like the sands by the sea that are way too many to count."' In our dire straits we are to take God's promises and turn them into prayer (as Alec Motyer would say); we plead the promises of God to which He must be faithful. What might this look like for us? It may mean that in this disease-ridden, saint-crushing, idol-chasing world, we pray that God will fulfill His Word to be 'exalted throughout the earth' (Ps. 46:10b). It may mean that we plead assurances like 1 Peter 5:10 ('The God of all grace who called you to eternal glory in Christ will see that all is well again; he will stabilize, strengthen and support you,' JB alt.), or 2 Corinthians 12:9 ('My grace is all that you need: my power is most fully displayed when my people are weak,' F. F. Bruce paraphrase). Do we wonder if we will be saved at the last? Can we not turn Jesus' word into pleading prayer – 'This is the will of the One who sent me, that I should lose nothing of all that he has given me, but raise it up at the last day' (John 6:39).

Third, *acknowledge His goodness* (v. 10) and do so confessing your unworthiness. 'I am unworthy,' Jacob admits, 'of all the loving acts and of all the faithfulness you have shown your servant.' Then he gratefully fleshes this out in saying, 'With my staff I crossed over this Jordan and now I have become two camps.' Gratitude should find its place even in crisis. I have heard distressed Christians do this. I visit or confer with them in their current trouble and then they begin to rehearse the kindnesses of God they have received and do have even in their latest distress. There's little more encouraging than hearing this testimony come tumbling out of them unsolicited – in the midst of their trouble.

Yogi Berra was the famous, all-star catcher for the New York Yankees baseball club in the late 1940s and 1950s. He grew up in St Louis in a close-knit Italian family. Years after his playing days he was in Los Angeles to tape a session of a radio or TV show he was doing. During a break, the taping crew were visiting, and the talk turned to parents. Someone asked Yogi about his and he took out his wallet and showed them photos of Pietro and Paulina, his father and mother. It was a bit too moving for one of the tech people – he began to tear up. 'How many 63-year-old men do you know,' he asked, 'who still carry pictures of his mother and father around with him?'[3] It was a subtle acknowledgement of how Berra prized

---

3. Allan Barra, *Yogi Berra: Eternal Yankee* (New York: W. W. Norton, 2009), p. 260.

his parents, an incidental indication of the debt of gratitude he owed them. So too our gratitude to Yahweh should always be right near the surface and scarcely a slip of the tongue away.

Fourth, *beg His help*. See how straightforward Jacob is in his request: 'Please deliver me from the hand of my brother, from the hand of Esau, for I fear him, lest he come and strike me down, the mother along with the children' (v. 11). No convoluted gymnastics in this prayer. Simply a precise petition, 'Please deliver me,' and a heartening candor, 'For I fear him.' How liberating that candor is – it tells me I can simply tell the Lord what is scaring me to death. Do we name our fears as honestly and truthfully?[4] Iain Duguid has said it well: 'You lay out all your fears before the Lord, ask him to do what he has committed himself to do in his Word, and then press on in faith.'[5]

Finally, this narrative forces us to consider **the place of calculated action** (vv. 7-8, 13b-21). What part does human activity play in all this dilemma – or ought it to play?

First off, Jacob takes action in face of cloudy circumstances (vv. 7-8). Esau is coming with 400 men. Does that mean Esau is going to attack? Or perhaps not – since he let the messengers go and return to Jacob? Was he perhaps playing with Jacob, simply making him sweat? Who can tell for sure? In any case, it seems that Jacob's action in verses 7-8 (splitting his entourage into two groups) was prudent and proper.

But what of the action Jacob takes after his prayer of verses 9-12? Next day, it seems, he assembles a 'present' for Esau

---

4. Cf. Calvin: 'For they who fancy that faith is exempt from all fear, have had no experience of the true nature of faith. For God does not promise that he will be present with us, for the purpose of removing the sense of our dangers, but in order that fear may not prevail, and overwhelm us in despair' (*Genesis*, 2:189).

5. Iain M. Duguid, *Living in the Grip of Relentless Grace* (Phillipsburg, NJ: Presbyterian & Reformed, 2002), p. 110.

(v. 13b). A rather substantial gift of over 550 animals. Jacob arranges these in distinct groups (v. 16), with instructions to his servants of what they are to tell Esau as each 'wave' meets him (vv. 17-20a). Clearly, his intention is to soften Esau up, to pacify him (v. 20b) with this stage-by-stage gift.

We can't be sure what else was in Jacob's mind because the text is silent about such. But IVP's *Bible Background Commentary* suggests some collateral purposes:

> Jacob's gifts to Esau demonstrate that he is as shrewd as ever. Besides being an attempt to gain Esau's favor through generosity, the continuous arrival of the herds of animals will wear out any schemes for ambush and deflate any degree of military readiness that Esau might be planning in his encounter with Jacob. Additionally, traveling with the animals will slow Esau down and make his company much noisier. Finally, the plan adds Jacob's servants to Esau's retinue—a decided advantage if there is to be fighting.[6]

Jacob may have had these very designs. But, as noted, it is very hard to be sure because the text does not explicitly tell us. We do know that Jacob meant 'to pacify' Esau by this serialized livestock transfer (v. 20b). That sounds a good bit like the old, calculating Jacob to me. And yet, surprisingly to me, Calvin is quite 'easy' on Jacob. He claims Jacob does not act distrustfully here:

> For though by prayer we cast our cares upon God, that we may have peaceful and tranquil minds; yet this security ought not to render us indolent. For the Lord will have all the aids which he affords us applied to use. But the diligence of the pious differs greatly from the restless activity of the world; because the world, relying on its own industry, independently of the blessing of God, does not consider what is right or lawful; moreover it is always in trepidation, and by its bustling, increases more and more its own disquietude. The

---

6. IVPBBC, p. 65.

pious, however, hoping for the success of their labour, only from the mercy of God, apply their minds in seeking out means, for this sole reason, that they may not bury the gifts of God by their own torpor.[7]

How are we to sort this out? I don't know that we have to do so, at least not in Jacob's case. We needn't debate pro-Jacob or anti-Jacob positions here. But we do need to use Jacob's case as a way of posing our own dilemma and of highlighting our need for discernment. If we were in Jacob's sandals and had prayed his prayer, would our livestock gift mean we were acting in faith or in place of faith? In our various quandaries we have to ask ourselves if our proposed action expresses faith or contradicts faith. Is our pathway prudence – the way faith should act? Or is it self-reliance, leaning on our own savvy and ingenuity?

There are two angles in such dilemmas. It reminds me of an exchange between a Federal soldier and his Confederate counterpart in the War Between the States. They were on picket duty for their respective camps on opposite sides of a river (likely in Virginia). Such pickets frequently kept up banter, sometimes with an edge. The Federal picket noted that his southern opponent on the other bank looked terribly ragged, so he called across, asking if the rebels didn't have any decent clothes. The Reb looked across at him for a moment and then called back: 'We-uns don't put on our good clothes to butcher hogs.'[8] Obviously, there were two ways of assessing shabby clothes! That is often our dilemma with human activity: does it demonstrate faith or deny faith? Naturally, we would prefer a sure-fire formula for sorting it out. But the best approach is probably the James 1:5 pattern:

---

7. Calvin, *Genesis*, 2:193.

8. Bruce Catton, *Glory Road* (Garden City, NY: Doubleday, 1952), p. 33.

'If any of you lacks wisdom, let him ask from the giving God ….' Or as the worship response goes:

Lead me, Lord,
lead me in thy righteousness,
make thy way plain before my face.[9]

9. *Trinity Hymnal* (1990), No. 727.

10

A GRACE COLLISION
(Genesis 32:22-32)

Once James Humes alleged that he had gone into a men's store in Philadelphia and when he asked the owner how he was, received the startling reply, 'Terrible, terrible. Monday, we had only one customer. Tuesday, we had none at all. And then Wednesday was worse than Tuesday.' That naturally brought on the query, 'How could Wednesday be worse than Tuesday when you had no customers on Tuesday?' 'Oh it was worse,' the owner shot back. 'The man who bought a suit on Monday came in and wanted a refund.'[1] What's bad can always get worse. It must've seemed that way to the lone figure pacing by the Jabbok[2] that night while his insides gnawed at him over meeting his brother Esau – that is until someone slammed into

---

1. James C. Humes, *The Sir Winston Method* (New York: William Morrow, 1991), p. 143.

2. We are left in logistical agnosticism about Jacob's location. Some think he was still on the north side of the Jabbok River after having sent family and goods to the south side (e.g., Steinmann); Currid suggests Jacob sends his family and goods back over to the north side of the Jabbok in order to place the semi-barrier of the river between them and Esau, who will be coming from the south; on this view, Jacob would've fought his opponent south of the Jabbok. We can't be certain.

him, sent him sprawling, and carried on an all-night brawl that lasted till nearly sun-up. There was one benefit: he stopped thinking about Esau.

Our passage is packed with conundrums. Who was the mysterious assailant? Why was he fighting Jacob? Why unable to defeat him? Why did he appear afraid of dawn coming? Why did he strike Jacob's thigh or hip? Why did he refuse to disclose his name?[3] In spite of these mysteries, I have called this segment 'a grace collision.' Am I importing this whole idea of grace here? But hasn't this been the theme even from the time Jacob left home? My father's short-hand definition of grace was 'something for nothing when we don't deserve anything.' Surely that is what we see in Yahweh's way with Jacob – it's clearly what we see and hear in 28:13-15 (especially in context of ch. 27). And there's the same gracious God speaking to him in 31:3, who protects him in 31:24, who encourages him in 32:1-2. But now, as he tries to enter the land, Jacob has been caught in a trauma sandwich – between Laban (ch. 31) and Esau (ch. 33). Laban is gone but Esau is coming. But before Jacob collides with Esau, he collides with God, with grace. Yet grace may be as agonizing as it is amazing; God can be gracious toward us without being nice; meeting a gracious God can be an ordeal. So what do we discover about grace here?

First, the text suggests that **grace may cripple you** (vv. 24-26, 31).

This section of the text presses several matters on us. One is *mystery*: 'so Jacob was left alone, and a man wrestled with him until dawn came up' (v. 24). There's Jacob and suddenly in the pitch of night hands grab him and fling him to the ground. Whatever we do with this, we must not say it was a vision or merely some sort of spiritual struggle or emotional conflict. It

---

3. These taken from Allen P. Ross, *Creation and Blessing* (Grand Rapids: Baker, 1988), p. 547.

was very physical – you don't go off limping on your hip (v. 31) from a psychological encounter. It *is* mysterious but we simply have to live with it. Then there's the matter of *identity*. Verse 24 says 'a man' wrestled with Jacob. But in verse 25 we are beginning to wonder, for when he saw he could not overcome Jacob, 'he touched his hip socket and Jacob's hip socket was strained while he wrestled with him.'[4] The verb 'touch' can also mean 'strike' and, as here, one has a dilly of a time deciding which nuance fits. If he 'struck' Jacob's hip, he gave it a good jolt and certainly reduced Jacob's abilities, but if he merely 'touched' it to produce such a result, we naturally wonder what sort of massive strength he has that a mere touch can disable like that. In either case, it seems, this opponent has such power that he could easily crush Jacob – unless he somehow chooses to restrain that strength. Then when Jacob refuses to release his opponent 'unless you bless me' (v. 26), he assumes he is grappling with the only One from whom blessing can truly come. And his assailant's statement in verse 28 suggests a divine adversary: 'you have fought *with God* and with men and you have won' (emphasis mine). Finally, when Jacob names the spot Peniel ('face of God') and explains 'for I have seen God face to face and yet my life has been preserved' (v. 30), there's little doubt that Jacob at least thought he had had a combat with deity.[5]

Besides mystery and identity we also meet with *tenacity* – that of Jacob (v. 26). 'I will not let you go unless you bless me.' Jacob's hip may be shot but his grip is not. He holds on

---

4. I am following Sarna here, who insists on 'strained' (or 'wrenched') rather than 'dislocated'; he notes that if Jacob's hip were dislocated, he would not even be able to limp (v. 31; Nahum Sarna, *Genesis: JPS Torah Commentary* [Philadelphia: Jewish Publication Society, 1989], p. 227).

5. Hosea 12:3-4 recalls Genesis 32: 'In the womb he grabbed his brother by the heel, and in his manhood he fought with God; so he fought with (the) angel and won; he wept and begged for grace.' The angel may well be a reference to 'the Angel of Yahweh,' who seems to be Yahweh Himself in His 'appearability' and accessibility to His people; Judges 6 and 13 are instructive on this.

for dear life. His opponent's request to be released (v. 26a) is likely for Jacob's benefit. If a too-close revelation of God could be fatal (cf. Exod. 33:20), and Jacob himself seemed to think so (cf. v. 30), then for Jacob's sake his opponent needs to be gone before light comes.

> God is not the one endangered by the daylight, it is Jacob! To see God in the full light of day would have meant death for Jacob. If Jacob holds on until daybreak, he is a dead man! At the same time, the continued grasping of God on Jacob's part in the near-dawn light also says something about Jacob. He is willing to risk death for the sake of the divine blessing.[6]

But Jacob doesn't care; he will hazard all if only to get blessing from the only source worth getting it from.

What then are we to make of this scene? The narrative tells us that when Jacob returns to the land he fears to face Esau but that God is his real opponent. Yahweh promised the land to Jacob and yet prevents his entry. Yahweh is Jacob's adversary. In the struggle He shows He could crush and decimate Jacob and yet permits him to fight on.[7] Here is a man who has made his way by trickery and deception, by conniving and self-sufficiency, and now this shadowy foe brings Jacob to the point where he wants Jacob to be: desperation. He brings him to the point of helplessness, where he realizes that blessing cannot come from his own plans and sweat and fast moves but only by begging and pleading for it from God. As Hosea 12 says, 'he fought with the angel and won; he wept and pled for grace.' That's a strange victory – weeping and pleading for grace. And the Lord left His mark: 'he went limping because of his hip' (v. 31).

---

6. T. E. Fretheim, 'Genesis,' NIB, 12 vols., 1:566.

7. One imagines accommodation operating here. Something like my playing tackle football with my sons when they were young. I could rough-house a bit with the ten-year-old, but was much more gentle when bringing down the six-year-old. One regulates the amount of strength one shows based on the capability of the child.

There's some 'spillover' from this passage for us. For one thing, this text helps smash a 'graven image' of God – the passive, waiting, gentlemanly One who waits for you to respond, who never imposes Himself upon you, for He is so democratic and believes in democracy as you do. No, this aggressive God takes the offensive and makes you fight with Him. Sometimes we hear that God will never force Himself upon you. Sorry – He will if He wants to.[8] We do not have a 'tame' God.

Again, the text teaches that sometimes God, in His grace, will oppose you, may 'cripple' you, in order to force you to face Him, so that you will have to struggle with Him, hang on for dear life, until you realize that only He can give you what you need. He does not oppose or cripple in order to destroy, crush, or mangle, but to get you to seek only Him.

J. C. Ryle knew something of this 'crippling' pattern. Ryle was that nineteenth-century, gospel-driven Anglican who could actually write short, pungent, non-flowery sentences! But when he was twenty-five years old (1841), his whole world caved in. He had been working in his father's banking business and it went bust. Ryle lost everything, didn't know where he would live or what he was to do. Had he not been a Christian, he said, he might have found suicide inviting. He said, 'If my father's affairs had prospered, and I had never been ruined … I should never have been a clergyman, never have preached a sermon, written a tract, or a book.' He went into the ministry because it was the only living open to him. He noted that had he not been ruined, he likely would have gone into Parliament and 'it would be impossible to say what the effect of this might have been upon my soul.'[9] So he was 'ruined' – grace 'crippled' him.

---

8. For another instance, see Exodus 4:24-26, and cf. my comments in *The Word Became Fresh* (Ross-shire: Christian Focus, 2006), pp. 67-69.

9. Iain H. Murray, *J. C. Ryle: Prepared to Stand Alone* (Edinburgh: Banner of Truth, 2016), pp. 49, 55-56.

Or go back almost one hundred years earlier to Scotland. Here is Hector M'Phail, minister at Resolis, and unconverted. He had married a Christian woman and perhaps she had not discerned he was unconverted. He was a minister, after all. At any rate, not long after their marriage, she told him on a Sabbath morning that her soul was starving, and she'd decided to go across to Kilmuir to hear the word of life from pastor Porteous. M'Phail made no objection; he even accompanied his wife to the ferry. But what a blow! To realize there was no nourishment in his preaching for his wife, that she had to go elsewhere. It pricked his conscience, he began to sense his unfitness for the ministry and went through a process of conviction for several years that led to his conversion.[10] What a blow, however, to hear one's wife say, 'My soul is starving,' and to stand and watch her ride the ferry to a ministry that would feed her, to realize the lethal deadness of one's ministry. Grace crippled in order to bring blessing.

Secondly, our passage tells us that **grace can fortify you** (vv. 27-32).

Where, then, does 'blessing' begin? For Jacob it begins with his name. 'What's your name?,' his antagonist asks. Then comes the confession: 'Jacob.' Then his opponent tells him that that will no longer be the case: 'Israel' will be his name. 'Sneaky' will be 'Victor.' Israel probably means 'God fights,' but note the spin the adversary puts on it when he explains the name, 'for you have fought with God and with men and have won' (v. 28b). He puts an idea-play on the verb so that Jacob is the fighter and winner. (Hosea would say he wins by weeping and begging for grace.) Jacob wants more – he wants to know his combatant's name (v. 29a) but that is not given. We have simply the statement, 'So he blessed him there' (v. 29b). I take

---

10. John Kennedy, *The Days of the Fathers in Ross-shire* (reprint ed., Inverness: Christian Focus, 1979), pp. 49-51.

that as a summary or recap statement. It does not point to a blessing in addition to the name change but simply points back to the name change as being or stating the blessing.

Names can reflect character or disposition. 'Nabal' means '(wicked) fool' (1 Sam. 25:25) and that's what he was; at least that's what Abigail his wife said, and she ought to know. Naomi told the chattering women in Bethlehem's gate not to call her Naomi (Pleasant) but Mara (Bitter) in view of the 'marring' God had brought on her. One can easily assume that Jacob's change of name signals a change in character, but I have come to doubt that. A name change can, for example, point to a coming change in circumstances (Gen.17:5), even though that may be years ahead. And here in Jacob's case, in view of the context (his fear of Esau, v. 11), the explanation of the name change functions *as the provision of assurance*. He has 'fought with God' and won. Is there anything scarier than that? If you win that one, can't you face anything? But he says, 'You have fought with God and with men.' Does the 'with men' include his upcoming encounter with Esau? If so, there's a sense in which that has already been won.

> This change significantly assures Jacob. If he can hold his own even with God, certainly he should be able to live up to his name with Esau.[11]

This assurance Jacob receives does not evaporate the goosebumps. Clearly he knows this fight could well have been fatal (v. 30). He has come out of it limping (v. 31) but alive. But let's cheat and read ahead. Jacob sees Esau and his 400 men coming (33:1). He takes precautions for his family that reflect his own favoritism (33:1b-2). But note: 'But he himself passed on in front of them' (33:3). No shrinking on Jacob's part. Grace gives guts. He walks straight ahead even if it may

---

11. Fretheim, p. 567.

be into a human buzz saw. After all, what can man hope to do to one who has been blessed by God Himself?

Jacob's experience was mysterious and frightening, but it's not as though it's light years removed from us. Hebrews 4:16 tells us we are to come near to the throne of grace so that we can 'find grace to help at just the right time.' Sometimes that grace is – as for Jacob – grace that fortifies us to face the next big fear. Simply because it's so down-to-earth I have always prized the story Bethan Lloyd-Jones told on herself. She was with her husband, Martyn, in his first pastorate in South Wales. One oppressive fear, kept to herself, haunted her. The south-west gales blowing in from the sea brought to mind how two former settlements (Aberavons) in that locale had perished. She bought a timetable of the tides, so she would know the times of the high tides. One night her husband was away; she was alone with the baby, a vicious wind blowing in from the sea. She said she was beside herself with fear, in panic, sleepless and tossing in her bed. What if the tide came up Victoria Road, she thought. Could she get out with the baby? Through a window? On to the roof? Finally, in simple despair, she got out of bed, on her knees and prayed: 'Lord, if it is all true, if you are really there and will answer my prayer, *please* give me peace and take all my fear away.' As she spoke, she says, it all went away. No more fear of gales and tides. Completely delivered and asleep in two minutes.[12]

You may think, 'My, that is dramatic and exceptional.' Is it? Or is it simply coming to the throne of grace to find grace at just the right time? Then that grace makes us able to wade right into our fears.

If you collide with grace, that is, with God in His grace, it should leave a lasting impression. You may discover that

---

12. Iain H. Murray, *David Martyn Lloyd-Jones: The First forty Years 1899-1939* (Edinburgh: Banner of Truth, 1982), pp. 238-39.

grace is as agonizing as it is amazing, as wrenching as it is wonderful. But you'll never fear an Esau if you've already wrestled with God.

11

'First be Reconciled to your Brother'
(Genesis 33:1-20)

Pretend you live in the American south where, in the warmer months, folks deem air conditioning a necessity. Let's say you have moved into a home in which the heating – air conditioning system is fifteen years old, original with the house, still functioning but a bit worrisome. Who knows whether it can operate through still another season? You decide to be pro-active, 'bite the bullet,' and fork over the inve$tment for a whole new HVAC system. So the company's service tech comes to your home to verify the size and sort of unit(s) they need to install and then he tells you that there will be no cost at all. It so happens, he says, that this will be the 500th HVAC unit his company has installed since its founding and that his boss had decided to mark such an occasion with free equipment and installation. You would likely feel like the sea had parted – saving $12,000 is almost inconceivable and yet it would be how you spelled 'relief' at that point. That too-good-to-be-true sensation is what we get as we walk into

Genesis 33. Let me draw attention to some observations that carry the teaching points of the text.

First, notice **the wonder of God's ways** (vv. 1-11). The first seventeen verses move from (1) preparation, vv. 1-3; to (2) reconciliation, vv. 4-11; and then to (3) negotiation, vv. 12-17. Here we are concerned with the first two components.

The air is electric – Esau and his 400 men are coming (v. 1). Jacob shuffles his family in line with his established scheme of favoritism (vv. 1b-2), and then, guts in place, goes in front of them all to meet Esau. Then the jaw-dropper: 'And Esau ran to meet him, embraced him, fell on his neck and kissed him – then they wept' (v. 4). Who could've imagined? Esau's curious. Who are these people (vv. 5-7), and why this livestock barrage I've met (vv. 8-11)? About the latter, Jacob is perfectly candid: 'to find grace in the eyes of my lord.' Is Esau's 'I have enough' (v. 9) typical polite banter? At any rate, Jacob insists, and Esau complies (v. 11). When Jacob calls his wave-upon-wave gift 'my blessing,' he may be thinking of a kind of restoration of the blessing he stole from Esau in chapter 27. But the big surprise is that the would-be murderer (27:41) has become a reconciled brother.

We see the wonder of God's ways here when we place chapter 33 next to chapter 31. How did God protect Jacob from Laban? He scared the wits out of him, threatened him, intimidated him (31:24, 29). Overt intervention was God's pattern in chapter 31. But that's not the way in chapter 33. On the one hand, God intimidates Laban, but on the other, He softens Esau (v. 4). Whether that was a matter of the moment or a process over time we can't tell, and it doesn't matter. God's work with Laban was overt and direct, whereas with Esau it was hidden and subtle. The God of the Bible seems to love variety, and when we see Him operating in such diverse ways, we should take warning not to try to box God in to one sort of procedure. His indirect and quiet ways are as much His work as His knocking Laban alongside his head.

Historian Stephen Ambrose relates a turning-point in his life. He was a sophomore at the University of Wisconsin. He was a pre-med student. He was going to follow in his father's footsteps. He naturally wanted to take biology, anatomy, and embryology, but the school held to certain basic requirements first. They forced students to take a history course. So, as he says, he just willy-nilly signed up for a required course in American history. He says, 'I walked in, and the professor – his name was William B. Hesseltine – had been talking about three minutes, and I wasn't a premed anymore.' He was a history major.[1] There was no trumpet fanfare – something simply happened inside in his consciousness, in his conviction. It was clear but quiet. That seems to be the way it was with Esau (v. 4). Sometimes God is blatant (with a Laban) and sometimes He is subtle (with an Esau). How delightful are the diversities of God's providence and how we should revel in the cornucopia of His ways!

The second matter I would call **the wobbliness of God's servant** (vv. 12-16). Esau seems to be all 'gangbusters': Let's pull out and get going and I'll lead the way (v. 12). But Jacob demurs, for plausible reasons: 'My lord knows that the children are fragile and the flocks and herds that are nursing weigh on me, and should they drive them hard, all the flocks will die' (v. 13). And so Jacob proposes Plan B: 'Let my lord pass on before his servant, and I will lead on more deliberately, in line with the pace of the cattle before me and in line with the pace of the children, until I come to my lord at Seir' (v. 14). That's a bit of a problem. Jacob, from the subsequent story, did not go to Seir to Esau's digs and likely had no intention of doing so, but he leaves the impression that he planned to do so. It looks

---

1. Brian Lamb, ed., *Booknotes* (New York: Random House, 1997), p. 54.

like the resurrection of the old conniving and deception that Jacob knew how to practice so well. Apparently, Peniel had not flushed all that out of his system.

Not all expositors hold to Jacob's deviousness here. Note that Esau proposes his own Plan B: he suggests leaving some of his men with Jacob to perhaps help him or apparently protect him on his journey (v. 15a). But Jacob nixes this as well. He says, 'Why is this? Let me find grace in the eyes of my lord' (v. 15b). Now it could be that this statement means something like, 'Why do that? Let's just drop the whole matter.' If so, Esau may have taken it as a request to dismiss it all, including any journey to Seir.[2] If so, it would be a rather obtuse way of expressing the matter. Hence I come down with those who see Jacob as reverting to his devious mode in implying he would come to Esau's turf.[3] That is the 'wobbliness' of God's servant. Post-Peniel we may have expected better from Jacob.

But is it all that surprising that Jacob still operates in the slippery mode? Who knows exactly why Jacob made this innuendo? Did he distrust the longevity of Esau's good will? For whatever reason he wanted to be free of him. Yet isn't this a pattern we see in the lives of so many of God's servants, even 'stellar' ones? At some point we see character glitches or behavioral glitches or disappointing inconsistencies that, given their allegiance to the Lord, should not be there.

You can see this in Martin Luther, for example. In his health-impaired later years Roland Bainton says he became 'an irascible old man, petulant, peevish, unrestrained, and at

---

2. Cf. B. K. Waltke, *Genesis: A Commentary* (Grand Rapids: Zondervan, 2001), p. 452.

3. Waltke holds that since the narrator himself does not evaluate Jacob's pose as deception, it cannot be viewed as such (Waltke, p. 452). But that won't wash. A writer need not evaluate or assess an action for it to be taken negatively. He might simply report it and expect his readers to have enough sense to see it for what it is. For the 'deception' view, readers can check, for example, the commentaries of Currid, Wenham, and Kidner.

times positively coarse.'[4] He refused even to recognize Zwingli and the Swiss reformers as Christians, and Luther's seeming deity-complex stirred the Swiss to deep anger. Oecolampadius said of Luther: 'Since he has lost control of himself, he believes that the greatest sin and the most unfair act in the world is to criticise him. We have here a miserable creature who smashes heaven and earth because we have told him that he too, as a man, might err ....'[5]

I don't dredge up Luther's case in order to excuse him. Such inconsistencies and harshness should have no place in Christ's servant. But there is need for patience. Ironically, in another connection, Luther himself counsels the same. While Luther was in 'exile' in the Wartburg for eleven months, the town of Wittenberg was sinking into chaos due to the influence of Carlstadt and others. Mobs would go round smashing Catholic altars, images, and shrines, smashing stained-glass windows. In desperation, town leaders appealed to Luther to return. He did, he preached, he calmed. He told the radicals who were trying to push reforms down the throat of the community that they needed to 'give people time.' It took him three years of study to see all that needed to be done. How can people be moved to welcome reforms in three months? You are wrong [he said]

> to think that you get rid of an abuse by destroying the object which is misused. Men can go wrong with wine and women. Shall we prohibit wine and abolish women? Sun, moon, and stars have been worshipped. Shall we pluck them out of the sky? Your haste and violence reveal a lack of confidence in God.[6]

---

4. Roland H. Bainton, *Here I Stand: A Life of Martin Luther* (reprint ed., Peabody, MA: Hendrickson, 2017), p. 388.

5. N. R. Needham, *2000 Years of Christ's Power*, 4 vols. (Fearn: Christian Focus Publications, 2004), 3:159.

6. Needham, 3:131.

So with Jacob and all God's servants. 'Give people time.' Not as though approving deviousness and inconsistencies. But we need to realize that believers do not drop out of some 'sanctification' chute with 'Refabrication complete' stamped on them. The lives of the Lord's servants may yet be laced with folly and foibles, and why should not Jacob be our teacher so we are not surprised or shocked at this? Taken in proper measure this point may prove of immense comfort to many of us.

The third keynote in our passage is **the word of God's promise** (vv. 17-18). However, first we must walk through a bit of geography and maybe a little speculation before getting to the meat of the matter.

After getting free of Esau, Jacob, perhaps turning north, comes to Succoth ('booths'), often identified as Tell Deir Alla, east of the Jordan, north of the Jabbok, near where it flows into the Jordan. Since Jacob built shelters for his livestock there and, apparently, a 'house' (v. 17), he must have settled there for some time. The condition of the livestock (vv. 13-14) may have called for some respite, not to mention his family. At some point after Succoth, he moved on west of the Jordan to Shechem, located about thirty miles north of Jerusalem (v. 18).

Are we to view Jacob's geography neutrally or negatively? A number of commentators see nothing blameworthy in Jacob's movements at this point. But Yahweh who had told Jacob to return to the land (31:3) had also called Himself 'the God of Bethel' (31:13) and recalled the solemn vow Jacob had made there (see 28:20-22). It seems that Bethel was the required and expected destination, but Jacob did not immediately enter Canaan but dithered at Succoth, and then must have planned to settle near Shechem. These 'stops' covered some years. A case can be made that Dinah, Jacob's daughter, was likely around six when they left Paddan-aram, but by Shechem-time in chapter 34 she is attractive enough that Shechem (Hamor's son) finds her irresistible. She would have been at least an early teenager (and her older brothers, sword-wielding guerillas). Why this Succoth-Shechem delay? Why so seemingly forgetful of his vow?[7] Maybe this tells us that we can have a life-transforming experience with the Lord (Gen. 32) and yet muck up the path of 'discipleship' afterwards.

I drag you through all that in order to stress that this text is not all sweetness and light and obedience. Yet in spite of all that, you must not miss the accent on *faithfulness* here. It's in verse 18 when it says Jacob came to Shechem, 'which is *in the land of Canaan*,' a clause that ought to be in blinking neon lights. And this means that the Lord has fulfilled His 'unlikely' promise of 28:15. It looked 'unlikely' because at the moment Yahweh spoke the promise Jacob was fleeing the land. In face of a scheming uncle and bickering wives and daily drudgery and threat of fraternal vengeance and some twenty years – 'through many dangers, toils, and snares' he is 'in the land of Canaan.' God's Word held firm, fast, and faithful.

No human promises, even when they look marvelous, can hold a candle to that. Once, after his retirement from major league baseball, Yogi Berra was in a golfing foursome that included President Gerald Ford. Berra mentioned that he owned a racquetball club in New Jersey, asked President Ford if he ever played such, discovered that occasionally he did, and so pulled a card out of his pocket and handed it to the President. Yogi said, 'Just in case you're ever in New Jersey and want to play racquetball.' The card said the

---

7. For some who see Jacob's locales negatively, see Derek Kidner, *Genesis* (London: Tyndale, 1967), pp. 171-72; H. G. Stigers, *A Commentary on Genesis* (Grand Rapids: Zondervan, 1976), pp. 255-56; and especially, Iain M. Duguid, *Living in the Grip of Relentless Grace* (Phillipsburg, NJ: Presbyterian & Reformed, 2002), pp. 125-27.

bearer was entitled to play racquetball at Yogi's club, free of charge. On the other side the card was stamped with: 'Good Tuesdays only.'[8]

That is not the way with Yahweh's promises. Human blundering (Jacob's or ours) does not negate them, changing conditions do not alter them, passing time does not erode them. And it's so delightful in the present text to see how subtle the writer is in expressing divine faithfulness. You would almost walk right by it if you weren't awake. It's hidden away in that sneaky little prepositional phrase, 'in the land of Canaan' (v. 18). He has made 28:15 come true.

It's not as if this is merely an ancient bit of biblical theology or an incidental chunk of Jacob's biography. We, as Jesus' disciples, have a vested interest in such fidelity, for this fidelity is hard-wired into the character of Jesus our Lord. Haven't you ever meditated on John 14:2 and simply let its implications wash over your spirit? 'In my Father's house are many dwelling places; if not, I would have told you' (HCSB). That is what we hang on to – the utter candor and absolute reliability of Jesus' word. Which is why we rest all our weight on His promise: 'If I go and prepare a place for you, I will come again and take you to myself, that where I am you also may be' (v. 3).

The final emphasis in this chapter focuses on **the worship on God's turf** (vv. 19-20). Yahweh had promised the land to Jacob and his seed (28:13). Now Jacob is back in the land but all he has of it is the plot he purchases from the locals at Shechem (v. 19). He paid one hundred *qesitah*; we have no idea what equivalent value that would be. But on that bit of land Jacob set up an altar as Abraham and Isaac had done (see 12:8; 13:18; 26:25). He names it, literally, 'God, the God of Israel' (v. 20). 'Israel' refers to himself, picking up the name

8. Allan Barra, *Yogi Berra: Eternal Yankee* (New York: W. W. Norton, 2009), p. 367n.

108

change Jacob had received at Peniel (32:28). The statement can also be translated, 'The God of Israel is God' (NET). If so, it is a confession of faith, implying that the God who changed his name and has been dealing with him is the true God. And he declares this via the altar in 'the land of Canaan' (v. 18).

This may seem like a miniscule matter, but it packs more importance than may be obvious. Something like the experience of Stan Telchin. Stan was Jewish and his and his wife's world had been blown apart when his college-age daughter told them she believed in Jesus as the Messiah. Stan went into his own quest to prove her wrong and in the process was drawn inch by inch toward Christian faith. He was still unconverted when he attended a large conference for messianic Jews at Messiah College. One morning Stan went to breakfast and someone (who didn't realize he had never confessed Christ) asked him to give thanks for the food. He did so and closed his prayer 'in the name of Jesus, the Messiah.'[9] It was only a phrase, only the closing of a prayer – but a small signal of a major change. Something like Jacob's altar. Not much perhaps, but by it Jacob is staking out a hunk of 'the land of Canaan' (v. 18) for 'the God of Israel.' There in the middle of Paganland was a piece of turf claimed for Israel's God.

Don't Christian believers do something similar in this world? It may not seem like much amid the scads of contemporary Canaanites. But when we worship in our homes – giving thanks for daily food, joining in morning and/or evening family worship, enjoying 'quiet times' of Bible reading and prayer, joining voices in singing psalms and hymns in the home – are we not in one sense claiming the turf where our home (or apartment) sits for the Lord of all the earth? It is one hunk of ground where Jesus now reigns. Across town

9. Scot McKnight with R. Boaz Johnson, 'From Tel Aviv to Nazareth: Why Jews Become Messianic Jews,' *Journal of the Evangelical Theological Society* 48 (December 2005): 779-80.

or countryside such spots may seem to be few, but they still keep breaking out like measles. They are small indicators that the time will come when '*the earth* will be filled with the knowledge of the glory of Yahweh as the waters cover the sea' (Hab. 2:14; emphasis mine).

12

COVENANT IN PERIL
(Genesis 34:1–35:8)

Lloyd George turned prophet when he summed up the 1919 Treaty of Versailles: 'All a great pity. We shall have to do the same thing all over again in twenty-five years at three times the cost.'[1] Who could conceive that the world would drop into another abyss of butchery after one world war? But it did. And, though Jacob's experiences were far cries from the scope of world wars, the repeating pattern is similar. He treacherously stole the blessing (ch. 27). That was one thing. But then he was caught in the clutches of Laban and the soap opera of Try-Living-with-Four-Wives (chs. 29–30). That was another. Enough. But no – now there's another mess: the scandal and deception and massacre at Shechem (ch. 34). It's as if Jacob is always crawling out of one pit and dropping into another. Genesis 34 is, of course, one of the nasty narratives of the Old Testament, but don't let the moral shock blind you to another problem it poses: there is a threat to the covenant itself here, a subtle threat to the covenant people. Maybe the prospect of

---

1. Cited in Marvin Olasky, *The American Leadership Tradition* (Wheaton, IL: Crossway, 2000), p. 205.

a little intermarriage, economic prosperity, and of becoming 'one people' (vv. 9-10, 16) won't seem too appealing. But what if it does?

We are getting ahead of ourselves. Let's settle down and look at chapter 34; we'll call it **covenant danger.**

You recall the story. Dinah, Leah's daughter, who must be in her teen years now, ventures out to 'see the daughters of the land.' Not a wise move unaccompanied. The son of the local head knocker saw her and 'laid her.' But Shechem's rape is not without some affection. He's infatuated with Dinah and longs to marry her. He demands that his father enter into negotiations with this Jacob group to that end. Shechem may have argued that his rape and expectation to marry Dinah already brought about a sort of *fait accompli* for joining the two groups. Jacob did nothing about it until his sons came in from their work. They had their own view of the matter – it was an 'atrocity' or 'outrage.' But likely Hamor (and Shechem) felt otherwise. Okay, so there was a forcible rape, but nothing a follow-up marriage couldn't set right – and surely Jacob's clan would be flattered to be tied to the leading local family. Shechem was simply itchy to plaster it up on Facebook.

Jacob's sons are chips off the old block – they answer 'deceitfully' (v. 13). Well, no, we couldn't possibly consent to this. Your male population would have to be circumcised as we are, and, if you don't agree to that, any of this 'one people' stuff is off. Hamor and Shechem see no difficulties. They make the pitch to their community: Just a small hitch, a little surgery, but think of what it will do for the economy (v. 23). Hamor and Shechem seem to assume that the Shechemites will be able to finagle a more lucrative benefit than Jacob and his family.

Circumcision is tougher on adult males than on eight-day-old male infants (cf. 17:12). So the whole male contingent of Shechem is debilitated, and, while they are 'in recovery,' Simeon and Levi (and doubtless their servants) go through the town, slaughtering all the helpless men. They make sure Hamor and Shechem meet their end, take Dinah away, and otherwise plunder the place, taking livestock, captives, and possessions. Vicious vengeance. Jacob complains. His is a pragmatic argument: now surrounding groups are likely to come in and crush his clan for this brutality (v. 30). Simeon and Levi respond with a 'moral' argument – Is it right for Dinah to be treated like a whore? (v. 31).[2]

Genesis 34, then, breaks down in an orderly sequence:

Transgression, vv. 1-7
Negotiation, vv. 8-17
Persuasion, vv. 18-24
Retribution, vv. 25-31

Now for some observations to keep in mind. First, this chapter is a 'godless' text – God is not mentioned anywhere in this story. Currid points out that the last verse of chapter 33 and the first verse of chapter 35 both refer to God, but there's nary a mention of Him in chapter 34. 'I believe this omission highlights the very secular and seedy nature of the present chapter.'[3] As if it's a quiet condemnation of all that happens here.

Second, like chapter 27, everyone is in the wrong. One can argue that Jacob was wrong in not proceeding to Bethel and instead settling down close to Shechem. Dinah was unwise in

---

2. Andrew Steinmann (*Genesis*, TOTC [London: Inter-Varsity, 2019], p. 326) says: 'They pointedly do not characterize her as "your daughter" but as *our sister*, once again bringing to the foreground the rift in Jacob's family.' Since Dinah was a child of the non-loved Leah (as were Simeon and Levi), it may be that Jacob had less concern for what happened to her. Wenham castigates Jacob here as 'a man whose moral principles are weak, who is fearful of standing up for right when it may cost him dearly, who doubts God's power to protect, and who allows hatred to divide him from his children, just as it had divided him from his brother' (*Genesis 16-50*, WBC [Dallas: Word, 1994], p. 318).

3. John D. Currid, *A Study Commentary on Genesis*, 2 vols. (Darlington: Evangelical Press, 2003), 2:147.

making her debut unattended. Shechem, in spite of his social status, is a scumbag for raping Dinah. Jacob seems bitten with the bug of moral lassitude (cf. v. 5), unable to see beyond pragmatic concerns (v. 30), and apparently functioning in line with his established favoritism (cf. v. 31; see above). Jacob's sons operate out of a pre-planned, conniving deceit (v. 13) and Simeon and Levi *et al.* inflict a bloodbath on helpless victims and satisfy their greed with plunder. 'There is none who does good.'

Third, and once more, we must distinguish between what the Bible *reports* and what it *supports*, between what it asserts and what it authorizes. Some folks, if they would happen on to Genesis 34, might raise a hue and cry, claiming that this is the sort of violence and viciousness the Bible approves. One tires, actually, of hearing such whiners and bellyachers, who without batting an eye will watch movies as, or more, violent than the nastiest biblical narratives. Yet one must constantly insist that because the Bible reports something does not mean it supports what it reports, that it does not necessarily delight in what it depicts. Rather, in the way it reports such events, it is clear that it abhors what it describes. We must keep the point in mind when dealing with a 'nasty' text like this.

Now what about this 'covenant danger'? All the wheeling-and-dealing and gruesome slaughter in the story can eclipse a subtle temptation. It comes in the guise of the invitation to Jacob and clan to become 'one people' (vv. 16, 22) with these locals. That's the pitch Hamor makes. Why allow a moment of forcible rape to become such a massive problem? Instead of making a moral mountain out of a social molehill, let's allow this rather unfortunate and rambunctious incident to become a kind of flagship episode that leads us into forming an integrated community:

Intermarry with us! You can give your daughters to us, and you can take our daughters for yourselves. And you can live *with us*, and the land will be open to you; stay and trade in it, and lay hold of property in it (vv. 9-10, emphasis in the text).

Yahweh later sounds the alarm about this very thing (Deut. 7:3-5). There's also been a concern about meshing with pagans in Genesis. Isaac must not be allowed to marry one of the Canaanite girls (24:3-4), nor must Jacob (28:1-2); indeed, already Esau's pagan marriages had brought much grief (27:46; cf. 26:34-35). Later, it looks like Judah had peeled off from his brothers and had decided to 'go Canaanite' (38:1-2). But could a local agreement reached within the confines of Shechem really have had much impact at all?

Such a question brings to mind the summer of 1816. On the other side of the world from the USA, the eruption of Mount Tambora in Java shot clouds of dust into the stratosphere that changed weather conditions even in the US. Americans in the northeastern US woke up to a twenty-inch snowfall. Those had probably occurred before, but not on June 6, as this one had. One would perhaps expect that what happened in Java would stay there or nearby, but it brought all sorts of zany and weird conditions to North America.[4]

Had that 'Integration Agreement' been confirmed at Shechem, it would have been 'curtains' for the covenant people. The temptation was there: think of the advantages; why be so distinct and stand-offish, when we can blend and coalesce? Do that and you will commit covenant wrecking (as later happened, Judg. 3:5-6) and covenant people will simply, sooner than you think, become mongrelized pagans, going around kissing wood and stone.

---

4. Larry Schweikart and Michael Allen, *A Patriot's History of the United States* (New York: Sentinel, 2004), p. 179. For further detail, Daniel Walker Howe, *What Hath God Wrought: The Transformation of America, 1815-1848* (New York: Oxford, 2007), pp. 30-31.

Contemporary covenant people are always facing this pull – not to be so distinct, to fit in with the current culture, to go with the flow. And, as in Genesis 34, nowhere is this danger more present than in the matter of our marriages. Christians can often suppose that it makes little difference if they marry unbelievers. As long as he or she is decent and attractive and not overtly opposed to one's profession of faith. And sometimes God is so gracious and rescues one from the mess he or she creates, perhaps bringing about the conversion of the unbelieving spouse. But more often than not, if you intermarry with unbelievers, with pagans, you may kiss your covenant with God good-bye and you will likely lose your children for God.

Our story continues into chapter 35, and here we see **covenant renewal** (35:1-4). Who knows what Jacob would have done, with everything discombobulated and in a shambles at the end of chapter 34? But God intervenes and gives direction: Get back to Bethel (35:1). The implication seems to be: fulfill that vow you made there at the first (28:20-22). So, he readies to set off to Bethel, a mere twenty miles south of Shechem on the spine of the central hill country.

There are two primary elements in this covenant renewal. One is *renunciation*. Jacob puts out the word: 'Put away the foreign gods that are among you, purify yourselves, and change your clothes' (v. 2). These images/idols were turned over and promptly buried there at Shechem (v. 4). One can't commit to the true God if one is still holding on to his false gods; the bandage is useless unless the wound is cleansed and washed.

We should not be at all surprised at the foreign gods among Jacob's clan. Rachel may have still had (and perhaps cherished?) her father's household gods (31:19, 34-35) and Jacob surely had a number of herdsmen and their families who clung to their traditional deities. But none of this should surprise us, as Steinmann reminds us.[5] This image/idol worship was universal religio-cultural practice. Who would think of worshiping a deity apart from an image? Everyone in the Near East worshiped by means of idols. Deities and images went together like cereal and breakfast. Anything else was weird.

We can't say Jacob himself had concrete idols. But a glance back at 34:30 suggests that perhaps peace and security had become an idol for him. Nothing wrong with wanting to secure security in a way – unless we cross a line and give it a supreme priority it ought not to have.

The other element in this renewal is *re-commitment*. One hears of it in verse 3 when Jacob says, 'Let's get up and go up to Bethel, and I'm going to make there an altar to the God who answered me in the day of my distress and has been with me wherever I have gone.' What a testimony those words are and what a shame that commentators don't spend more time with them! What a God to worship! One who has heard his cries and delivered him in his distresses and who never left his side in all the slop he went through. This God of verse 3 is the death-knell to idolatry, for if one really has a God like verse 3b, why would one ever want to mess with idols?

Not long ago I was preaching on this passage at a conference. It was just after my next-door neighbor had purchased a new lawnmower. Now I should say that when we moved into our current home, I bought a John Deere lawn tractor in order to cut my yard. Our lot is about six-tenths of an acre, and I was not excited about spending eight hours behind my 22-inch push mower in order to mow my grass. Hence the lawn tractor. It's not exactly the in-thing, but riding it and mowing with it gives me the illusion of 'farming.' But Chris, my next-door neighbor, had just bought a slick, bright orange, Kubota zero-

---

5. Steinmann, p.327.

turn mower, with a 48-inch width cut. Those zero-turns are all the rage with some fellows. Now do you suppose he would be tempted to have my John Deere when he has that Kubota super-job? I doubt it. And if one has a God like Jacob's (v. 3b), why would one want to mess with idols?

This back-to-Bethel movement has some overspill for Christian believers. Isn't this covenant renewal something we should be practicing not once but repeatedly? Shouldn't this be the way the Lord's supper functions for us? A 'Bethel' where we lay aside our most recent idols or our crass self-sufficiency (Rev. 3:17) and renew our love to the Lord who answers us in our distress and sticks with us in them all, a time when

> Jesus calls us from the worship
> of the vain world's golden store,
> from each idol that would keep us,
> saying, 'Christian, love me more.'[6]

Finally, one must not pass up the note of **covenant protection** in this text (35:5-8). As if in answer to Jacob's fears (34:30), verse 5 tells us, 'Then they traveled on and a terror from God came over the cities that were around them, and they did not pursue the sons of Jacob.' So Jacob gets safely to Bethel and builds his altar (vv. 6-7). This 'terror from God,' whatever it was, sounds a bit like God's intimidation of Laban in 31:24, 29. Sometimes the Lord puts the strait jacket on His people's enemies, in this case by scaring them stiff. They were clamped in heaven's vise.

---

6. From a hymn by Cecil Frances Alexander; *Trinity Hymnal* (1990), No. 591. Sadly enough, in some of our churches the Lord's supper is not a conducive time for believers to renew their commitment to the Lord. Sometimes the reason is that the minister talks too much and little time is given for quiet and silence (why do they think they must always play music?) for saints to do business with their Lord; see the recent reprint of Jacob Jones Janeway, *Meditations on the Lord's Supper* (Madison, MS: Log College Press, 2021), pp. xii-xiii.

But it all seems so 'wrong.' After all, we haven't forgotten chapter 34. These are the moral delinquents who wiped out and plundered a defenseless people – and set them up for it by deception. They ought to be run down and run over. Why is God giving particular protection to such reprobates who don't deserve it? But there's part of the problem. Where would God find people who 'deserve' it? Seems like God is acting in grace again, and one wonders if sometimes God doesn't have to bear shame for acting in grace.

Yet it's more than that. It all goes back to the 'quad' promise in Genesis 12. There were four (hence 'quad') elements in that promise to Abram/Abraham:

People	(great nation, 12:2; seed, 12:7)
Place	('the land,' 12:1b; 'this land,' 12:7)
Program	('in you all the families of the ground will be blessed,' 12:3b)
Protection	('I will bless your blessers, and the one who despises you I will curse,' 12:3a)

Yahweh is simply abiding by the protection-clause of His promise (cf. Ps. 105:12-15). He has pledged Himself to preserve His people, His undeserving, foolish, sinful, knuckle-headed people. That is why Jacob's clan receives protection here. It's also why there is still a people of God in this world today.

I do not usually find communists amusing, but I have always enjoyed Molotov's rejoinder to Ribbentrop. It was late 1940 and the Russian was in Berlin, conferring with the Nazi regime. The German position seemed to be that the beginning of the end had now arrived for the British empire. Britain was done for; it was only a matter of time till she would admit her defeat. The talks ranged over all sorts of matters, not least how to parcel out various territories. One evening during the talks, supper was served at the Soviet Embassy, and after supper there was a British air raid on Berlin.[7] Sirens blew, and all the brass and not-so-brass moved to shelters. Molotov and Ribbentrop entered the latter's own shelter and carried on their discussions. Ribbentrop once more pontificated on how England was finished and was now nearly helpless. To which Molotov logically replied: 'If that is so, why are we in this shelter, and whose are these bombs which fall?'

Yes, exactly. It is one thing to say these people don't amount to anything and another to ask why they are still here anyway. And the church often appears in her sin and foibles and weakness – and yet she is still here. That is because of Genesis 12:3a – it's part of the ammunition the Lord loaded into His promise.

---

7. Churchill implies that the Brits knew of these meetings, were miffed that they weren't invited, and so decided they would put in an appearance! Cf. Churchill's *Their Finest Hour* (Boston: Houghton Mifflin, 1949), pp. 579-84.

13

THE MIXED BAG OF COVENANT LIVING
(Genesis 35:9-29)

Imagine a six-year-old lad who's ill and has to go to the local clinic and see the family doctor. That doctor may sport a white coat and our lad may see him consulting with and inquiring of various patients. But sometime later the boy is walking down the street in his neighborhood and sees the doctor on a ladder, cleaning the leaves out of the gutters on his house. A few days later he sees him with the hood (bonnet) of his vehicle up and he's checking the oil level in the engine. And it hits our six-year-old that though the doctor may be the head man at the clinic, there are yet common, every-day tasks he also must tackle. That's sort of the impression 35:9-29 leaves. I suppose we could call this section 'From Bethel and Beyond,' seeming to be a collection of notes and anecdotes closing off the Jacob narrative. In their own way they show that living in covenant with God does not always mean dramatic deliverances or tense tales of fear, faith, and failure – it also deals with pretty basic, earthy matters.

First, then, the text implies that **covenant people walk through common troubles** (vv. 16-21, 22, 27-29). Looking at the last segment first, verses 27-29 show that some troubles are expected. Jacob arrives at Hebron. Who knows how long he was there? But there Isaac died, and Esau and Jacob buried him. Sad, to be sure, but not a shock. They knew they could expect to lose Isaac eventually. But what happened earlier on the way from Bethel to Bethlehem was another matter. Rachel died from complications in child-birth (vv. 16-21). Rachel, the love of Jacob's life. Rachel, who had asked for another son (30:24), had been granted him (v. 17) but not the time to enjoy him. Ben-oni, 'son of my sorrow,' indeed. Jacob buried her somewhere along the road to Ephrath (Bethlehem) and specially marked her burial spot (v. 20). Then we read simply, 'And Israel traveled on …' (v. 21a). What else could he do? Only put one foot in front of another and go on.

These 'common troubles,' however, can prove even more wrenching than bitter losses (like Rachel's death) – sometimes they consist of tragedies driven by human sin. 'And while Israel dwelt in that land, Reuben went and had sexual relations with Bilhah, his father's concubine; and Israel heard (about it)' (v. 22a). Israel heard and he didn't forget (49:3-4). The note is so terse – one wonders if the writer is so disgusted, dismayed, or ashamed over it that he cannot bring himself to supply any details. He is loath to describe it; he can barely bring himself to mention it.

What might Reuben have been trying to bring about? He was not likely driven by sexual lust (Bilhah would've been a good bit older than he). Bilhah was Rachel's maid, and so 'by violating Bilhah, Reuben makes sure that she cannot supplant or even rival his mother's [Leah's] position of chief wife now that Rachel is dead.'[1] Since Reuben 'laid' her, she would be 'damaged goods.' Or, Reuben may have been lusting

---

1. Nahum M. Sarna, *Genesis*, JPS Torah Commentary (Philadelphia: Jewish Publication Society, 1989), p. 244. Sarna has a very useful discussion, pp. 244-45.

after power or position. By violating one of Jacob's wives he was making a claim to family leadership, a move to usurp Jacob's position. This, at any rate, seems to have been the idea when one claimed a king's harem, as Absalom did in later years (2 Sam. 16:20-22).[2] It is one thing when a pagan assaults Jacob's daughter (ch. 34), but now his son commits incest with one of his wives. Human sin ravages and shames the covenant people.[3]

So sorrow, grief, and death are part of our 'common troubles.' Covenant people get cancer, have strokes, and are injured and killed in traffic accidents. We have no exemption card. God is forming a special people for Himself here in the text but in this story the Holy Spirit makes sure we know of some graves along the way (one can add Deborah's in verse 8). We are not sticks and stones, not some sort of third thing or some kind of macho-humans impervious to such ravages. To be sure, some believers lose their loved ones and can be radiant and 'victorious' at such times. But often that is not the case. And I'm tempted to say it does not have to be the case. Often you may go home and sob and shake and weep over your loss. You do it again on Tuesday morning and when you wake up in the middle of the night – and again on Friday morning. Even three months later (when you feel like you've gotten a bit of a 'hold' on yourself), while you're standing and singing 'Praise to the Lord, the Almighty' in worship, you suddenly tear up and off you go again. Maybe it was that stanza that went, 'How oft in grief, hath not he brought thee relief.' Faith does not insulate us from sorrow. It is, literally, a grave matter. We too lose our Isaacs and Rachels.

---

2. See my *2 Samuel* (Ross-shire: Christian Focus, 1999), p. 207; also J. Robert Vannoy, *1–2 Samuel*, Cornerstone Biblical Commentary (Carol Stream, IL: Tyndale House, 2009), pp. 370, 372-73.

3. I am skeptical of some of Calvin's exposition here. I think he goes over the top in claiming Reuben was 'born again by the Spirit of God' (*Genesis*, 2 vols. in one [reprint ed., Edinburgh: Banner of Truth, 1975], 2:247).

Some of our common troubles, however, are Reuben-like – they are caused by sin in our family connections. These can prove more grievous than losses by death. These obviously may not be like Reuben's offense, though some may be in that category. Sexual abuse occurs in professedly Christian families. A father or stepfather sexually abuses daughters in the household and mars and scars their lives for years to come. Or there's a son or daughter who has professed faith and seemed to be walking with Christ and suddenly announces that he/she has renounced that faith. Think how brokenhearted Theodosius Harnack must have been over his son. Adolf von Harnack was a popular and much-lauded church historian in the late nineteenth and early twentieth centuries. But he thought Christ was a human being just as we are and denied He was God in the flesh. For him the gospel was the fatherhood of God, the brotherhood of man, and the value of each individual soul. So at one point Theodosius Harnack told his son:

> Our difference is not theological, but rather one which is profoundly and directly Christian. Thus if I would ignore it, I would deny Christ as he who views the resurrection as you do, is in my view no longer a Christian theologian.[4]

For Harnack's father, apostasy was not a noun but a tragedy.

Or what of John Calvin? Antoine was his younger brother whose wife Ann had been caught in adultery with Calvin's servant Pierre. Then about five years later (1562) Calvin's stepdaughter Judith (daughter of Idelette, the widow Calvin married), who had a glowing reputation, stood before the consistory and confessed to adultery.[5] Was there shame in

4. Cited in John D. Woodbridge and Frank A. James III, *Church History Volume 2: From Pre-Reformation to the Present Day* (Grand Rapids: Zondervan, 2013), pp. 554-55.

5. Thea B. Van Halsema, *This Was John Calvin* (Grand Rapids: Baker, 1981), pp. 210-11.

that for Calvin? Undoubtably. But more than that – grief and anguish over what had been done. There are sorrows, as losses from death. But there are *sadder* sorrows – the tragedies that sin brings. So in our covenant families and fellowships we face the pregnancy out of wedlock, the son or daughter who insists on marrying an unbeliever, one who claims she is now a lesbian, a widowed parent who decides to 'move in' with a new partner, a son who flaunts his new agnosticism all over his Facebook page.

A great number of us know these kinds of heartbreaks. There's such a helpful realism in Old Testament narrative. It is not shy to say there may be a 'Reuben' in our family circle. Even rather tedious texts have their value: they keep us from thinking we can live in some sort of victory-in-Jesus La-La-land. And that's a plus.

There is even another plus in this piece of narrative because it tells us, secondly, that **covenant people receive divine assurance** (vv. 9-15, 22b-26). Verses 9-15 relate the overt assurance Jacob received when God appeared to him at Bethel. A good bit of this assurance consists of reassurance, especially of the *people* aspect of the promise (v. 11) and the *place* aspect (v. 12). I like what Griffith Thomas said about verse 9a ('God appeared to Jacob again'): 'How striking is this word "again"!'[6] I find it striking because it suggests how keen God is to assure His servant. The Lord had already appeared to and encouraged Jacob along the way (28:10-22; 31:3, 11-13; 32:1-2, 22-32; 35:1). Now He 'again' appears and assures him. It seems He never tires of putting fresh heart and certainty into the souls of His servants.

Then there is more assurance here, but it is not overt but subtle, and it is not for Jacob but for the readers of Genesis (well, they are the ones who can see how it functions in the literary

---

6. W. H. Griffith Thomas, *Genesis: A Devotional Commentary* (Grand Rapids: Eerdmans, 1946), p. 333.

context). It's found in a list (vv. 22b-26), which usually makes the most tedious reading. We find little fascination with lists. People who do, well, you know, such folks tend to be a bit odd. But you must see what this list of Jacob's twelve sons is saying to us, and it's saying it in the face of Rachel's death (vv. 16-21) and Reuben's incest (v. 22a). Seems like it implies something. Well, the covenant people are not yet the sand by the seashore (22:17; 32:12), nor are they like the stars in the sky (15:5), but twelve sons is a lot more than one (ch. 21).[7] Here then is a picture of Yahweh's *interim faithfulness.* And like it often does, it comes in the most plain wrappings (a list). It stands there rather silent, as if to say, 'Up to this point, Yahweh has helped us' (1 Sam. 7:12).

Sometimes God's assurance is quiet, hidden, restrained, like this. Donald Grey Barnhouse told of a man who, before the days of refrigeration, operated an ice house. He lost a very fine watch in that icehouse, somewhere among all the sawdust. He offered a reward and men went through the sawdust with rakes, without success. When they left the building for lunch, a small boy went into the icehouse and came out in a few minutes with the watch. They asked him how he had done it, and he told them: 'I just lay down in the sawdust and listened, and finally I heard the watch ticking.'[8] That's the way this list of sons is here – it's buried among the sorrows and sins of Jacob's family but points to the so-far faithfulness of God to His people promise. Sometimes that's what you need to do: look and listen carefully among all the trash and gunk of life and see tucked away the silent, steady, unfailing faithfulness of God toward you.

---

7. The implication is similar to Genesis 29–30, the tempestuous fertility fiasco and yet eleven sons at the end of it all. By the way, 35:26 says these sons were born to Jacob in Paddan-aram and, obviously, Benjamin (v. 24) was not; but the writer is speaking generally and not pedantically – there is no need to nitpick at his statement.

8. Donald Grey Barnhouse, *Let Me Illustrate* (Westwood, NJ: Fleming H. Revell, 1967), p. 119.

14

THE REST OF THE STORY

Paul Harvey used to have a radio program under the slogan, 'The Rest of the Story.' He would relate some account of an event or of a person's experience and then (after the commercial) tell the surprising or unexpected ending, the rest of the story. I'm a bit reluctant to take Jacob's story beyond the bounds of his 'own' narrative in chapters 25–35. I know he figures frequently in the next chapters of Genesis but I've no intention of going through those passages in detail. Chapters 25–35 contain the *toledoth* of Isaac (25:19), the story or accounts that develop from or after Isaac, and those primarily involve Jacob. But the *toledoth* of Jacob (37:2) doesn't focus on Jacob but on what develops from Jacob and so the focus is on Joseph and his brothers. Nevertheless, I think it might be helpful to survey these later chapters of Genesis and make some final observations regarding Jacob; it might serve as a useful summary and give closure (as the professionals like to say) to our study.

Notice, first of all, **the flaw he retains** (42:38). The scene here takes place during the famine, between the two times the brothers go to Egypt to get grain. The 'Food Czar' in Egypt had demanded the brothers bring back with them their youngest brother (Benjamin) when they next returned (Simeon had been held as collateral). Jacob flatly nixed the very idea: 'My son will not go down with you; for his brother is dead, and he alone is left, and should harm come to him on your journey, you shall bring down my gray hairs with sorrow to Sheol.' Interesting. Maybe we shouldn't be too picky. But he says, 'My son,' not 'your brother'; he says, 'his brother,' not 'your brother'; and then, 'he alone is left' – as if Benjamin is the only one who counts now. Looks like Jacob is still displaying the blatant favoritism he has always shown. He doesn't seem to conceal it. The other brothers don't count for much.

This favoritism has a long history. Seems to have started with Isaac and Rebekah, with Isaac pro-Esau and Rebekah pro-Jacob (25:27-28). It probably owes something to Leah's being deceptively pawned on Jacob (29:23-25) and it was no secret how Jacob regarded Leah (29:30-31). Even though she was the most 'prolific' wife, her stigma would likely attach to her sons. Even in the line-up for meeting Esau (33:1-2), it was no secret whom Jacob prized the most. Then when Dinah was raped (34:2), Jacob kept quiet about the matter till his sons came in (34:5). Was that because it was a 'family matter' for all to weigh in on, or was it partly indifference, because, after all, Dinah was Leah's daughter? Certainly her brothers seem irate over Jacob's scale of values (34:30-31).

This pattern, then, of who counted and who didn't was already established. It simply fully hits the fan in chapter 37. If Jacob knew of the animosity of the brothers against Joseph (and would he be so dense as not to know?), why would he send Joseph on a Go-and-check-up-on-your-brothers mission (37:14)? The brothers allow their hatred to spring a slow leak – enough to make money off him rather than murdering him. But that required the Dothan-gate cover-up (37:31-35). Fast forward to famine time and the first trip to Egypt and Jacob keeps Benjamin home – he is too valuable to risk (42:4). Then there's 42:38. 'He's the only one left!' Naturally, that could mean the only one of Rachel's children left; but the brothers could've sensed that it meant he was the only one who really mattered.

Here then is this attitude that persists in Jacob's life, and he never seems to alter it or ameliorate it. Sometimes people are like that. Ambrose Burnside was a Union general in the War Between the States. He was a reasonably humble fellow and had every reason to be. At the Battle of Sharpsburg (Antietam) he was ordered to get his men across to the west side of Antietam Creek. There was a road running parallel to the creek which then turned west over a bridge. Georgia sharpshooters were picking off a number of his men in their attempts to cross. Burnside was fixated on the bridge, sending men again and again into that obvious danger. Imagine how irate some of his men were later when they checked the creek. It was barely thigh-deep in most places – they could have forgotten the bridge, crossed over *en masse* and driven off the sharpshooters. But Burnside stuck to the same old plan. About four months later at Fredericksburg, Burnside sent his troops against a fortified Confederate position on Marye's Heights. Union corpses and wounded were piled high. It was sheer slaughter, 13,000 Union casualties. But next morning Burnside was going to renew the assault! Only the objections of some of his underlings kept him from repeating the same tragedy. He had this way of simply doing what he had done before.[1]

That's the way Jacob was with his favoritism. I'm not saying that Jacob made no progress in faith; but sometimes there can be folly that persists and tags along in God's servants. We seem to fall into it again and again. We know that sanctification is not a one-shot, microwave experience. But sometimes we should perhaps wonder if we are making any progress at all.

---

1. Clint Johnson, *Civil War Blunders* (Winston-Salem, NC: John F. Blair, 1997), pp. 113-14, 129.

We easily have our 'favorite' pitfalls, which need not drive us to despair but should at least drive us to prayer – that we might gain a heart of wisdom and by grace attack the trouble.

Move on to 46:1-4. Jacob has just been staggered with the news that Joseph is alive and ruling in Egypt (45:26-28). The text doesn't tell us, but we still wonder: Did Jacob's sons now confess what they'd done to Joseph? 'Oh, Dad, we better tell you that we've been deceiving you all these years, since you thought Joseph had been mauled to death [37:33]; actually, here's what happened ....' But the writer has bigger fish to fry: he focuses on **the assurance he receives.** At Beersheba, the jumping-off point for the journey to Egypt, God speaks to Jacob in a vision at night. He began with: 'I am the God, the God of your father; don't be afraid of going down to Egypt' (46:3a). For all his anticipation of seeing Joseph, Jacob likely had some reservations. One perhaps can't be sure if Jacob himself knew all that we know from Genesis, but Abraham had hatched a fiasco by going to Egypt (12:10-20), Jacob's father Isaac had been explicitly warned not to go there (26:2), and there may have been the shadow of coming and extended suffering in another land (15:13) that hung over one's thinking. There's no reason for concern 'for,' he says, 'I will make you into a great nation there' (v. 3b). As if the Lord says, Egypt will not be a path away from the promise but a way into it; precisely there is where I will fulfill the *people*-aspect of the promise. Then comes the best part, the *protection* (or, presence) aspect of that promise: '*I* will go down with you to Egypt, and *I* will surely bring you back' (v. 4). The first-person pronoun is emphatic. Jacob's God is a 'mobile' God; He is not shut up in Canaan. If He can 'go' to Mesopotamia (28:15), He can surely handle Egypt as well.

I fear I've kept hammering this assurance-theme on readers, but that's because the text keeps pummeling us with it. The living God seems to know how acutely His people stand in need of assurance. Perhaps we're a bit like that elderly woman

Herbert and Lou Henry Hoover had to deal with. World War I was about to explode in Europe and the Hoovers were working feverishly to get American tourists stranded in England back to the USA. They dug up money for them, booked passage for their return; Mrs. Hoover saw to food, lodging, and some entertaining diversions for the women and children while they waited to leave. They found room for this one elderly lady on a ship bound for the US, but she demanded a written guarantee that it wouldn't be sunk by submarines! So they gave her one![2] Did it really guarantee anything? No, but you can see how desperate this woman was for assurance.

Doesn't David celebrate this 'Jacob assurance' of God's presence in Psalm 139? Whether we venture to Egypt or arrive in Sheol (139:8), Yahweh is there. And you can tell from the tone of the psalm that David can hardly get over it. No depth is too deep (139:8), no distance is too far (139:9-10), no darkness is too dense (139:11-12) to keep Yahweh out. 'I will go down with you into Egypt' (46:4) doesn't fill in all the details – it only deals with what matters.

Third, let's listen in on the 'Pharaoh interview' (47:7-10) and notice **the candor he displays.** Pharaoh asks Jacob how old he is ('the days of the years of your life'). Jacob in reply calls his life 'my sojourning' at first rather than 'my life.' He tells Pharaoh his life-span to date is 130 years. Then in the rest of verse 9 he offers Pharaoh an editorial comment on his life. In that comment he uses the adjective *ra'* to describe his days. It is often translated 'evil' – 'few and evil have been the days ....' And the word does mean bad or evil, but not necessarily indicating what we might call moral evil. It can connote distress or misery. I think that is the sense here. Jacob is saying, 'Few and nasty have been the days of the years of my life' (v. 9b). You might expect Jacob to spruce it up a bit for

---

2. Paul F. Boller, Jr., *Presidential Wives* (New York: Oxford, 1988), p. 274.

Pharaoh, but he tells it the way he sees it. Life has pretty much been nothing but trouble, Pharaoh. Sarna has tallied it well:

> The biographical details of Jacob's life read like a catalogue of misfortunes. When he was finally able to make his escape and set out for home after two decades in the service of his scoundrelly uncle, he found his erstwhile employer in hot and hostile pursuit of him. No sooner had this trouble passed than he felt his life to be in mortal danger from his brother Esau. Arriving at last, at the threshold of Canaan, Jacob experienced the mysterious night encounter that left him with a dislocated hip. His worst troubles awaited him in the land of Canaan. His only [?] daughter, Dinah, was violated, his beloved Rachel died in childbirth, and the first son she had born him was kidnapped and sold into slavery, an event that itself initiated a further series of misfortunes.[3]

If Jacob's one-liner is hyperbole, it is accurate hyperbole.

There's something attractive about such candor, maybe because it's so rare. I found an instance of it in Agatha Christie's autobiography. Agatha's father had died; she was eleven; her mother was inconsolable and was not 'coming out of it.' The extended family had the brilliant idea that Agatha should be their emissary to rehearse to her mother the usual gibberish people pass on as consolation. So poor Agatha went in and approached her mother's bed, and, touching her timidly, said, 'Mummy, father is at peace now. He is happy. You wouldn't want him back, would you?' Suddenly her mother reared up in bed, and cried in a low voice, 'Yes, I would, I would do anything in the world to have him back – anything, anything at all. I'd force him to come back, if I could. I want him, I want him back *here*, now, in this world with *me*.'[4] There's something

---

3. Nahum M. Sarna, *Understanding Genesis* (New York: Schocken, 1966), p. 184.

4. *Agatha Christie: An Autobiography* (New York: Bantam, 1977), p. 102. This was a bit shocking for young Agatha. But her mother quickly told her, 'It's all right, darling. It's all right. It's just that I am not – not very well at

so refreshing about candor like that – refusing to imbibe the usual pablum folks trot out at such times.

Now Jacob's candor was certainly true. Well, whether his days at 130 were few, they had certainly been 'nasty'. A great deal of that nastiness had been of Jacob's own making. Many of the Lord's people down through the years could use Jacob's statement as a description of their own earthly pilgrimage, ones who were not primarily or necessarily responsible, like Jacob, for their misery and distress. And sometimes they leave their candor on record.

Surely John Calvin's life and ministry were by no means unfruitful, nor was it true that he never had any joy. But he freely confesses the 'nastiness' of his days in Geneva. Before he and Farel were thrown out of Geneva in 1538, Calvin says of those days: '[I]f I were to tell the least part of the cares, or rather the miseries, which we were forced to endure throughout a whole year, I am sure that you would think it incredible. I can assure you that not a day has passed in which I did not ten times wish for death.'[5] After three years Geneva was sinking in chaos and asked Calvin to come back. Are we surprised at his reaction? 'I would rather submit to a hundred other deaths, than to that cross on which I would have to perish a thousand times every day!'[6] You might accuse Calvin of hyperbole, though maybe not, when you remember he was afflicted with arthritis, migraines, stomach bleeding, bowel disorders, hemorrhoids, kidney stones, fever, muscle cramps, and gout.[7]

---

present. Thank you for coming.' Her mother kissed her and she went off consoled. A nice combination of frankness and kindness.

5. J. H. Merle D'Aubigné, *History of the Reformation in Europe in the Time of Calvin* (reprint ed., Harrisonburg, VA: Sprinkle, 2000), vol. 6, p. 395.

6. N. R. Needham, *2000 Years of Christ's Power*, 4 vols. (Fearn: Christian Focus Publications, 2004), 3:220.

7. Needham, 3:227.

The point here is not to suggest we should form a cult of folks who can feel miserable about their lives. It is rather to say that Jacob was gratifyingly straight-forward in assessing the hardship of his life and we should not feel compelled to airbrush away that reality if it's a huge chunk of our own. I know believers who face acute and ongoing physical pain day after day. And that affliction does not include the disappointments and losses they have also endured along the way. Shouldn't they have freedom to be truthful? 'Few and nasty have been the days of the years of my life.'

If Jacob is candid, he is not morose. That brings us to the last observation: **the testimony he leaves** (48:11, 15-16). If Jacob is candid before Pharaoh, he is grateful before Joseph. He reflects on what God has brought about and says, 'I never expected to see your face, and, my!, God has even allowed me to see your seed' (v. 11). Joy really did come in the morning (Ps. 30:5).

I think we hear Jacob's testimony best, however, in what he says about God. And that comes as part of His blessing on Ephraim and Manasseh, Joseph's sons. He begins with:

> The God before whom my fathers Abraham and Isaac walked, the God who has shepherded me all my life to this day, the Angel who has rescued me from all disaster, may he bless the lads (vv. 15-16a).

Thanksgiving blends with testimony. 'The God who has shepherded me,' who has cared for him, defended him, sustained him, disciplined him, stayed beside him. 'The Angel who has rescued me' is also a reference to the Lord. In 31:11 'the Angel of God' reveals Himself as 'the God of Bethel' (31:13). But has He, did He really 'rescue [Jacob] from all disaster'? Well, here Jacob still is, talking about it. It is quite a record – to be preserved from Laban and Esau and peril and possible attack at Shechem and from famine (41:57–42:2). Perhaps the best clue to a man's faith is what he says about his Lord as he looks back over his life. It's often very moving as well.

I found this to be so when I recently re-read one of Charles Hodge's letters to his brother. Hodge taught biblical studies and theology at Princeton Seminary for many years. He was the youngest child in his family. Three older siblings died very young; his brother Hugh and Charles were the only surviving children. The year after Charles was born, his father died; his mother was a widow with a toddler and a six-month-old. And now, years later, near Christmas of 1867, Charles wrote to his brother Hugh:

> Should I live another week I shall be seventy years old. You have already passed that boundary. When we look back over this long period, how much cause for gratitude meets our view. What a Mother we had to watch over our infancy and train our youth, and secure for us, at such sacrifice to herself, a liberal education. God has preserved us from wasting or disabling sickness. He has granted us a good measure of professional success and usefulness. We have children who are our joy and delight; all of them the professed and consistent disciples of our blessed Lord; all promising to be useful in their several vocations. Their mothers, after having been spared to us for many years, as inestimable blessings, are now safe in heaven. And we are still blessed with health and the use of all our faculties, surrounded and sustained by those who look upon us with respect and love. Above all, God has given us a good hope through grace of eternal life beyond the grave. Who of all our acquaintance can recount such a catalogue of blessings?[8]

What a delightful testimony! Not one that all of us can share in every particular, for God's providences have been different with many of us. But still a testimony, like Jacob's, of a shepherding and redeeming God all his life long.

---

8. A. A. Hodge, *The Life of Charles Hodge* (1880; reprint ed., Edinburgh: Banner of Truth, 2010), pp. 521-22.

Back to Jacob's testimony. He speaks of the Angel who 'rescued' him. The noun or participle *go'el* (sounds like: go-ale), rescuer, is cognate to the verb used here. At least later in Israel's life it referred to the male relative or family friend who came and bailed a family member out of debt or slavery.[9] Jacob's 'Angel' has been such a rescuer – and that from 'all evil.' That's the usual translation. But, again, the word has a wide range, covering evil, harm, distress, misery, disaster. Here I have translated it 'disaster' – 'the Angel who rescued me from all disaster.' Well, 'disaster' pretty well sums up Jacob's life. He was, after all, God's **rascal**. But the Shepherd and Angel 'rescued [him] from all disaster.' He was, after all, **God's** rascal.

---

9. Cf. G. J. Wenham, *Genesis 16–50*, WBC (Dallas: Word, 1994), p. 465.

FAITH
OF OUR
FATHER
EXPOSITIONS OF GENESIS 12–25
DALE RALPH DAVIS

ISBN 978-1-78191-644-5

FAITH OF OUR FATHER

Expositions of Genesis 12-25

Dale Ralph Davis

With typical wit and wisdom Dale Ralph Davis opens up chapters 12-25 of Genesis. These beautiful and insightful expositions guide you through some of the early chapters of the Bible and will deepen your understanding of this important area of Scripture which helps shape our understanding. This is an ideal resource for pastors as well as small groups and personal study.

> ... another example of the lively biblical exposition that readers of Dale Ralph Davis have come to know and love ... Anyone wanting to study, preach, or teach Genesis 12-25 will want to have this book ready at hand.
>
> SCOTT R. SWAIN,
> Professor of Systematic Theology, Reformed Theological Seminary,
> Orlando, Florida

> Ralph Davis is probably my favorite Old Testament expositor: he always unfolds the text with freshness, insight, and humor, leaving the reader with a clear understanding of what God is up to and the difference that should make in our lives. This volume on Abraham is a classic in the making!
>
> IAIN DUGUID,
> Professor of Old Testament, Westminster Theological Seminary,
> Philadelphia, Pennsylvania

THE WAY OF
THE RIGHTEOUS
IN THE
MUCK OF LIFE

Psalms 1–12

MUCK OF LIFE

Dale Ralph Davis

ISBN 978-1-78191-861-6

The Way of the Righteous in the Muck of Life

Psalms 1-12

Dale Ralph Davis

In the opening pages of the Psalms, believers discover foundational truth for right living-and great delight – as children of God. Trusted theologian Dale Ralph Davis leads readers through a careful study of Psalms 1-12 with clear application for daily life.

The Psalmist begins with the most essential truth for mankind, Davis explains: 'Nothing is so crucial as your belonging to the congregation of the righteous.' And it is the Word of God that provides the direction for the believer's life. It is here, Davis points out, that 'the righteous man gets his signals for living.' The delight of the righteous is in the 'law' – the teachings – of the Lord. Indeed, for those who belong to Him, meditating on God's Word is 'the pursuit of pleasure'! The Psalms are a treasure trove for such a pursuit.

As the first 12 Psalms continue, we see basic principles unfold with great clarity. Much like our troubles today, the Psalmist endured wickedness all around, a world hostile to the true God – and on a very personal level – deceit and persecution from his enemies. Readers are pointed toward the glorious rule of the Messiah, to whom the whole world belongs. In light of this realization, we are prepared to face all kinds of troubles that cause despair. The righteous rely on God, and the Psalms teach us how. This book is ideal for use by small groups, as a teaching guide or for reference.

SLOGGING ALONG IN THE PATHS OF RIGHTEOUSNESS

Psalms 13-24

Dale Ralph Davis

ISBN 978-1-78191-304-8

SLOGGING ALONG IN THE PATHS OF RIGHTEOUSNESS

Psalms 13-24

Dale Ralph Davis

Dale Ralph Davis plunges right into the middle of King David's hard times with a study that is resonant for our lives. King David's faith brought him through the muddy parts of life. Will we find that depression is our final response to a hard path? Will faith carry us across?

Find the encouragement that Psalms 13-24 hold for the Scripture-filled life.

Thank you Dr. Davis, for 'yielding to the temptation' to continue what you began with Psalms 1-12.

ALBERT N. MARTIN
Served as pastor of Trinity Baptist Church, Montville, New Jersey for over forty years and taught Pastoral Theology at the Trinity Ministerial Academy

Sharp, personal and funny illustrations, a vital, earnest and readable style, deep, nourishing, practical application built on a foundation of passionately thorough biblical, theological and linguistic scholarship.

COLIN BUCHANAN
Christian children's recording artist and author, Sydney, Australia

Always fresh, always insightful. Dale Ralph Davis shows you what's there and leaves you wondering why you didn't see it before!

COLIN S. SMITH
Senior Pastor, The Orchard, Arlington Heights, Illinois and President, Unlocking the Bible

Christian Focus Publications

Our mission statement –

STAYING FAITHFUL
In dependence upon God we seek to impact the world through literature faithful to His infallible Word, the Bible. Our aim is to ensure that the Lord Jesus Christ is presented as the only hope to obtain forgiveness of sin, live a useful life and look forward to heaven with Him.

Our books are published in four imprints:

CHRISTIAN
FOCUS

CHRISTIAN
HERITAGE

Popular works including biographies, commentaries, basic doctrine and Christian living.

Books representing some of the best material from the rich heritage of the church.

MENTOR

CF4•K

Books written at a level suitable for Bible College and seminary students, pastors, and other serious readers. The imprint includes commentaries, doctrinal studies, examination of current issues and church history.

Children's books for quality Bible teaching and for all age groups: Sunday school curriculum, puzzle and activity books; personal and family devotional titles, biographies and inspirational stories – because you are never too young to know Jesus!

Christian Focus Publications Ltd,
Geanies House, Fearn, Ross-shire,
IV20 1TW, Scotland, United Kingdom.
www.christianfocus.com